289.8 Sa55
Sanchez, Anita, 1956-
Mr. Lincoln's chair

D1028327

Mr. Lincoln's Chair

The Shakers and Their Quest for Peace

You never will kill the Devil with a sword.

— Ann Lee

Executive Mansion,

Washington, *August 8th, 1864.*

My good friends:

I wish to express to you my cordial thanks for the very comfortable chair you sent me some time since, and to tell you how gratefully I appreciate the kindness which prompted the present.

And I must beg that you will pardon the length of time that, through an oversight in my office, has elapsed without an acknowledgment of your kindness.

I am very truly
Your friend & obt servt.
A. Lincoln

To the Community of Shakers
New Lebanon Springs
New York

Frontispiece. During the height of the Civil War, the Shakers sent Abraham Lincoln a gift — one of their exquisitely crafted chairs. The Shakers deeply appreciated Lincoln's support of legislation that would recognize the status of conscientious objectors. Lincoln sent them this letter of thanks, personally signed, on August 8, 1864. Use courtesy of Shaker Museum and Library, Old Chatham and New Lebanon, NY.

Mr. Lincoln's Chair

The Shakers and Their Quest for Peace

by

Anita Sanchez

illustrations by

Joan Jobson

The McDonald & Woodward Publishing Company
Granville, Ohio

289.8
Sa55

The McDonald & Woodward Publishing Company
Granville, Ohio

Mr. Lincoln's Chair: The Shakers and Their Quest for Peace

Text © 2009 by Ana Maria Sanchez
Line illustrations © 2009 by Joan Jobson

All rights reserved.
First printing March 2009
Printed in Canada by
Friesens, Altona, Manitoba

10 9 8 7 6 5 4 3 2 1
18 17 16 15 14 13 12 11 10 09

Mixed Sources
Cert no. SW-COC-001271
© 1996 FSC
FSC

Library of Congress Cataloging-in-Publication Data

Sanchez, Anita, 1956-
  Mr. Lincoln's chair : the Shakers and their quest for peace / by Anita
  Sanchez ; illustrations by Joan Jobson.
    p. cm.
  Includes bibliographical references and index.
  ISBN 978-0-939923-94-6 (alk. paper)
  1. Shakers—United States—History. 2. Shakers—United States—Politics
and government. 3. Pacifists—United States—History—19th century. 4.
Pacifism—Religious aspects—Shakers. 5. Lincoln, Abraham,
1809-1865—Relations with Shakers. 6. United States—History—Civil War,
1861-1865—Religious aspects—Shakers. 7. Shakers—United States—Social
life and customs. I. Jobson, Joan. II. Title.
  E184.S53S26 2009
  289'.8—dc22
                                                              2009005948

Reproduction or translation of any part of this book, except for short
excerpts used in reviews, without the written permission of the
publisher is unlawful. Requests for permission to reproduce parts of this
work, or for additional information, should be addressed to the publisher.

Kent Free Library

iv

Table of Contents

For my mother

Mr. Lincoln's Chair

The Shakers and Their Quest for Peace

Introduction

Abraham Lincoln, as soon as he began his four tumultuous years in the White House, received sacks of correspondence — piles of letters, invitations, and gifts. Many Americans felt almost a personal connection to the lanky, awkward man in his ill-fitting clothes, who seemed more accessible than his tightly-buttoned predecessors — more like one of the folks. Lincoln's presidency coincided with the widespread use of photography, and his homely face, topped by a shock of thick, untidy hair, was as familiar to most people as that of their next-door neighbor. Abraham Lincoln seemed like someone with whom they could lean over the fence and have a chat.

Armchair generals sent the president advice on strategy, offers of amazing inventions that would infallibly win the war, or scoldings for military blunders. Missives from heaven arrived, personally signed by the Angel Gabriel. Romantic ladies besieged him with reams of patriotic poetry and requests for locks of hair; office-seekers begged shamelessly for favors; bitter pleas for justice came from African-Americans. Lincoln disregarded, with apparent cheerfulness, the frequent arrival of profane or violently specific death threats.

Gifts sent by Lincoln's admirers ranged from the humble to the magnificent: a pair of hand-knitted socks, a pen-wiper, a "Mammoth Ox, [named] General Grant."[1] To Lincoln's weary secretaries, there seemed no end to the stream of offerings: a pair of live eagles, an embroidered sofa cushion, a case of wine (although Lincoln was a tee-totaller). A polite offer of war elephants came from the King of Siam. Many presented Lincoln with food: pineapples, half a dozen hams, a fresh salmon, fruitcake. One thoughtful gentleman sent a cure for indigestion.

One day, yet another gift arrived at the White House, addressed to the president. It was a wooden chair.

Perhaps the harassed secretaries scratched their heads at the sight of this unadorned piece of furniture, suitable for kitchen use. The chair must have looked oddly out of place in the nineteenth-century White House, which was furnished along the lines of Buckingham Palace, with gold and crimson hangings, velvet draperies, and frescoed ceilings. Noah Brooks, a contemporary visitor, described furniture lavishly upholstered in blue and silver satin damask. "The woodwork of the chairs, sofas, etc., [is] solidly gilt," he continued admiringly. "Broad mirrors, with massive frames, surmount the marble chimney-pieces."[2]

In contrast to all this magnificence, the chair stood, plain and solid, designed with a strange, spare elegance. The simplicity of its design could not hide the craftsmanship: every rung straight, every joint polished and perfect, down to the smallest detail. The chair was basically the classic New England slat-back that had been common in American homes since Pilgrim days, but master craftsmen had taken this form and pared it to the bone, sternly resisting the temptation to add any trimmings. The man who was born in a log cabin may have found something refreshingly familiar in its simplicity.

The chair was a large one, to fit a large person; it was doubtless designed with the six-foot-four Lincoln's long legs in mind. The president pronounced it a "very comfortable chair."[3]

The empty chair stood in the president's office: a silent ambassador. It was sent to Mr. Lincoln by a unique group of people — some of the strangest non-conformists our nation of non-conformists has ever seen. Abraham Lincoln hailed these folk as "my good friends," but most Americans were suspicious of their bizarre religious services, during which the worshippers would dance, sing, and shake with fervor when they felt the Holy Spirit.[4]

Their formal name was "The United Society of Believers in Christ's Second Appearing." But the defiant Believers had taken an insulting label the World stuck on them, and adopted it as their own; they were proud to be known as "the Shakers," feeling that their faith was "indeed mighty enough to shake the heavens and the earth."[5]

～

My own first encounter with the Shakers didn't begin with a chair — it began with a lamp, hanging in the polished hallway of a Shaker Dwelling House. The lamp looked old-fashioned, with a wick in a basin and a large funnel over the top, but a sleek metal tube poked out of the side, stretching overhead to a vent in the wall. It seemed an awkward contraption, a strange blend of old and new.

"The tube removes soot and smoke," the tour guide explained. "Shakers were concerned about breathing clean air."

I looked back at the lamp with amazement. As an environmentalist, I know that air pollution is a worldwide crisis, with far-reaching consequences for the entire planet. The Shakers were ahead of their times, I thought approvingly. But as I explored further, I discovered that this was just the tip of the iceberg.

At first glance, the restored Shaker village had seemed a drowsy corner of rural New England. But as I wandered the grounds of the living history museum on that sunny October afternoon, I grew more and more aware that something earth-shaking had once gone on in this tranquil place. It seemed that every detail of life had been examined, and reinvented, by the Shakers. Their picturesque barn was designed like a Swiss watch, planned to ease the labor of the workers and ensure the well-being of the animals. Rustic workshops housed heavy-duty power tools: circular saws, an industrial-sized washing machine. These peaceful farmers had literally built a better mousetrap — a "have-a-heart" trap. I began to wonder — who in the world were these people called Shakers?

These ingenious inventors were not of "the World" at all. The Shakers were — and are — a group of religious non-conformists who withdrew from society, which they called the World, and dedicated themselves to a life of worship interspersed with labor. Their villages were not unlike Catholic monasteries, and like monks and nuns, Shakers were strictly celibate. Shakerism was one of the many Utopian "experiments" of America's early days. And that's what first drew me to the Shakers — their role as daring experimenters.

They were always ahead of their times, these strange people. They constantly tried new things: techniques to improve health, inventions to lighten work. They sought, with a passionate idealism, to make the world a better place — in fact, to make a perfect heaven of a very imperfect earth.

They would not have called themselves scientists, of course, but like true scientists, they questioned everything. Shakers examined the familiar trappings of life — a lamp, a broom, a wash-tub — took them apart, and experimented. And when they put things back together, they created something new.

But the Shakers didn't stop with redesigning lamps and improving brooms. They looked at the social conventions of their time, and relentlessly took them apart as well. They redefined the concept of family; they reinvented God. They tossed aside the ordinary rules of life and made up their own. "Tell them," cried Ann Lee, the Shakers' founder, "that we are the people who turn the world upside down."[6]

In their tranquil villages, Shakers turned their backs on the World's values, its politics, and especially its wars. Shakers were among the very first Americans to reject violence; they took their stand as conscientious objectors in the nation's earliest days. Beginning with Mother Ann's defiance of Revolutionary War officers, Shakers have battled with authorities for the right to abstain from war.

In the nineteenth century, the Civil War hit the nation like a freight train, and the Shakers were in its path. After two years of bloodletting, horrendous casualty lists had made it all but impossible to attract volunteers. Shaker Brothers, like many unhappy men before and since, were receiving messages from their draft board.

Never afraid to question authority, the Shakers decided to take their protest right to the top. That image — the Shaker Elders walking into the White House to inform Abraham Lincoln that they had no intention of fighting in his "uncivil war" — captured my imagination.[7] What did these most peaceful of people say to the commander-in-chief of the nation's bloodiest conflict? How did the president respond to American citizens who refused to vote, and denied that they were a part of "the World?"

And does this story — this long-forgotten footnote to history — have any value for us today? What we can learn from the Shakers, it seems to me, is their passion for never-ending and fearless experimentation. We, too, can challenge authority; we, too, can re-invent the rules. The Shakers showed us that we don't have to do things the way they've always been done.

We don't have to breathe polluted air. We don't have to waste so much time on household chores. We don't have to raise our food on factory farms.

And maybe — just maybe — we don't have to go to war.

Notes

[1] Holzer, Harold. *Dear Mr. Lincoln; Letters to the President.* Reading, MA: Addison-Wesley Publishing Company, 1993, p. 222.

[2] Brooks, Noah. *Lincoln Observed: Civil War Dispatches of Noah Brooks.* Baltimore, MD: The Johns Hopkins University Press, 1998, p. 82.

[3] Abraham Lincoln to New Lebanon Shakers, August 8, 1864. In the collections of the Shaker Museum and Library, Old Chatham, NY.

[4] Ibid.

[5] Sprigg, June. *By Shaker Hands.* Hanover, NH: University Press of New England, 1975, p. 8.

[6] Bishop, Rufus, and Seth Youngs Wells, compilers. *Testimonies of the Life, Character, Revelations and Doctrines of Our Ever Blessed Mother Ann Lee, and the Elders with Her; through whom the Word of Eternal Life was Opened in this Day of Christ's Second Appearing: Collected from Living Witnesses, by Order of the Ministry, in Union with the Church.* Hancock, MA: J. Tallcott and J. Deming, 1816, p. 318.

[7] Clark, Thomas D. *Pleasant Hill in the Civil War.* Lexington, KY: Pleasant Hill Press, 1972, p. 25.

A Place Where It
Is Always Sunday

September 16, 1863

Henry Blinn opens the door of the Dwelling House, steps out onto the porch, and closes the door behind him. He is a lean figure, plainly dressed in a drab coat and trousers; a pleasant-faced young man, with a long, thin nose and thoughtful, observant eyes (Figure 1).

In the fresh September morning, Canterbury Village spreads out around him. Maple-shaded paths are lined with the familiar buildings: the schoolhouse, the infirmary, the carpenter shop, the laundry. The workshops are painted a quiet gray, while the Meeting House glows pure white.

From the Dwelling House porch, Henry Blinn can see far over the gentle green landscape, where a wide sky stretches over pastures and fertile fields. In the orchard, the apples are ripening and the bee-hives are filled with their sweet harvest. But today there is no time to pick fruit or collect honey. This peaceful New Hampshire village has been his home since childhood, but now it is time to leave.

He settles the flat straw hat on his head and sets off down the Dwelling House steps. Morning birdsong sounds from the rustling maples. Although it is not the Lord's Day, a Sabbath serenity fills the air, for Henry's beloved home is a Shaker village, "a place where it is always Sunday."[1]

Figure 1. At the time of the battle of Gettysburg, Henry Blinn had been a Shaker for a quarter of a century. Use courtesy of Shaker Museum and Library, Old Chatham and New Lebanon, NY.

The Brothers and Sisters move purposefully along the paths, headed to their separate tasks in field and workshop. From the Dwelling House kitchen comes a whiff of cinnamon and apple — the pies are in the oven. But he will not be there for dinner.

Once he leaves the shelter of the tightly-clustered buildings, a strong mountain wind flaps his coat-tails and threatens to steal his hat. He strides swiftly down the path, for he has a train to catch — he has to hurry — he mustn't be late. On an ordinary week-day, Henry Blinn would have been about his ordinary tasks. This versatile man has many trades: school-teacher, tailor, carpenter, bee-keeper, dentist. But just now he has no time to teach the children or craft a chair. Today he has an urgent appointment to keep.

Three weeks ago, he had received the following message:

Form 39
Provost Marshal's Office.
2nd District of New Hampshire

August 21, 1863

To Henry C. Blinn
Canterbury, N.H.

Sir:

You are hereby notified that you were on the 19th day of August, 1863, legally drafted into the service of the United States for the period of Three years, in accordance with the provisions of the act of Congress, "for enrolling and calling out the national forces, and for other purposes," approved March 3, 1863.

You will accordingly report, on the 16th of September, at the place of rendezvous in Concord, N. H. or be deemed a deserter, and be subject to the penalty prescribed therefor by the Rules and Articles of War."[2]

Notes

[1] William Hepworth Dixon, in Stein, Stephen. *The Shaker Experience in America.* New Haven, CT: Yale University Press, 1992, p. 222.

[2] Blinn, Henry. *An Historical Record of the Society of Believers in Canterbury, vol. 1, New Hampshire.* In the collection of Canterbury Shaker Village, Canterbury, NH, 1892, p. 298.

The Slaughter Pen of the Nation

The volunteers are pouring in, to join the fight for freedom,
 To swell the ranks of Union blue, and nothing can defeat'em.
One nation and one flag, we say, whomever war may slaughter!
 We're going down to Richmond town, to fight for Abraham's daughter.

— Traditional Civil War song

Not far from Canterbury, another small town drowsed in the calm of a country summer. Gettysburg, Pennsylvania, was also a place of neatly-swept doorsteps, well-filled barns, and roads lined with rustling trees; as tranquil, apparently, as Henry Blinn's Shaker village. But on a hot summer day in that memorable year of 1863, the inhabitants of Gettysburg heard the rumble of cannon fire. Over the course of three days, their lawns and pastures were covered with dying men; the wheat-fields were sown with corpses, the fruitful orchards soaked in blood.

After the battle, the armies moved on, leaving the town's citizens to deal with the aftermath — thousands of dead bodies putrefying in the summer sun, mounds of amputated limbs. More than twenty thousand wounded and dying soldiers were left behind for the townsfolk to bandage, nurse, and feed — or bury. In August, when Henry Blinn received his draft notice, there were still many graves to dig. The little town of Gettysburg had become one vast cemetery.[1]

More than half a million Americans died in the Civil War. When Lincoln first called for volunteers in the spring of 1861, going off to fight had seemed like a fine adventure. Thousands rushed to enlist for ninety days, afraid the war would be over before they had a chance to fight. In the first summer of the war, elegantly-dressed spectators and congressmen from Washington thronged the battlefield at Bull Run, eager to watch the fun — and then got more excitement than they bargained for when they had to skedaddle out of the way of advancing Confederate troops.

Enthusiasm faded. It soon became apparent that the war was going to be a long drawn out affair. The terms of enlistments now were for a period of years, not days. Soon casualty lists mounted to terrifying proportions. By 1863, after two years of bitter struggle, the conflict still showed no signs of ending. Lee's defeat at Gettysburg in July of that year put an end to Southern hopes of imminent victory, and meant that the war could drag on indefinitely.

Today, everyone knows who won the War Between the States, and in hindsight, the result of history seems inevitable. But in the midst of the conflict, the outcome was by no means clear. The weary and harassed president of the war-torn Union was often despondent about the future. "We are now on the brink of destruction," Abraham Lincoln told a friend, after yet another disastrous defeat for the North. "It appears to me the Almighty is against us, and I can hardly see a ray of hope."[2]

But to the inhabitants of Canterbury, these were distant events. Henry Blinn, hearing of the bloodshed occurring in orchards and pastures very like his own, put it in agricultural terms; he wrote with deep disgust of the "slaughter pen of the nation."[3]

Canterbury Shaker Village in New Hampshire, Henry Blinn's home, was one of almost twenty Shaker establishments in the eastern United States. The Believers worked and worshipped together, their self-sufficient villages a world unto themselves. However, Shakers were willing to keep on good terms with their neighbors. They paid their taxes promptly, never protesting that their religious status should make them exempt. They were good neighbors indeed, contributing money or produce from their fertile farms to those in need — but they kept to themselves. Most Shakers generally had little contact with non-Shakers, though some Brothers traveled far afield to peddle Shaker wares, and carefully chosen Elders were designated as "Trustees" to handle necessary dealings with outsiders.

The World's people frequently passed by these prosperous, tidy, enigmatic Shaker villages. Curious folk peered over the white-washed picket fences with suspicion, contempt, or envy. They scratched their heads and asked the same question we find ourselves asking today: Who *are* these people called Shakers?

In a museum of American crafts, there stands a row of beautifully designed chairs, lined up side by side. Each chair is different, but each is made with the hallmark Shaker excellence. Shaker craftsmen sometimes designed a piece of furniture for the person who was to use it, and it's not hard to imagine the individuals, now long dead, who once sat in these chairs.

First in the row is a short-legged rocking chair, broad of seat and easy-going. Beside it, a narrow chair has a straight-backed, tight-lipped look. One long-legged chair has a handy drawer under the seat, for a busy Sister to store her sewing. Another has a "tilt button" on the back legs, so that a careless Brother could lean his chair comfortably back and not mar the floor.

Historians often state that "Shakers did this," or "Shakers believed in that," implying that all Shakers were exactly alike. Outwardly, they could indeed appear similar — their style of dress allowed little expression of individuality. But under the plain straw hats and identical white caps, the Shakers were as different from each other as are any cross-section of humans — some passively followed the rules, others broke them; some were brilliant, articulate, and learned, others illiterate; some were joyous, some melancholy, others stern and uncompromising. There was no such thing as a typical Shaker.

Similarly, no two Shaker villages were exactly alike, and customs, attitudes, and rules could vary from place to place. Shakers have existed for more than two hundred years, and it's important to remember that the Shaker of the 1700s was very different from the Shaker of the 1800s, or from the twenty-first-century Shakers who still exist.

But some qualities the Shakers must have shared. They were people for whom ordinary life was not enough. Since the Believers were celibate, no one was born a Shaker — even the orphans raised in their villages were given a choice when they reached adulthood, whether to go or to stay. The people who became Shakers chose their own path.

It was not an easy road. Some, like Henry Blinn, joined the Believers in spite of the horrified warnings and pleadings of their families. Those who persevered and signed the Shaker Covenant made the decision to turn their backs on the World, to leave behind home and family; they relinquished all their worldly goods, and dedicated their souls and their bodies to Shaker life.

At the time of the battle of Gettysburg, Henry Blinn had been a Shaker for a quarter of a century. He had spent a good part of his childhood, and his entire adult life, on the quiet Canterbury hilltop. To Elder Henry, the tens of thousands of the World's people who were blowing each other to bits on the green Pennsylvania fields must have seemed like lunatics.

But the violence, apparently, had nothing to do with him. He had not even voted for Abraham Lincoln — since Shakers did not vote at all. The War of Southern Secession must have seemed as distant from Canterbury Shaker Village as the wars in the Old Testament — the remote happenings of another time and place.

But all of that was about to change.

Notes

[1] Historians estimate that there were approximately fifty thousand casualties at Gettyburg, the war's bloodiest battle. Casualty statistics include those killed, wounded, and missing. Casualty figures for the Civil War are much debated, and it's hard to pin down the precise human cost of a battle, since some of the wounded died days, weeks, or even years later, and the fate of "missing" soldiers is difficult to determine. Estimates here and elsewhere in this book are from Livermore, Thomas L. *Numbers and Losses in the Civil War in America, 1861–1865.* Bloomington, IN: Indiana University Press, 1957.

[2] Orville Hickman Browning, quoted in Donald, David Herbert. *Lincoln.* New York, NY: Simon and Schuster, 1995, p. 403.

[3] Blinn, *Record,* vol. 1, p. 192.

Sweet Shaker Life

Come life Shaker life,
Come life eternal,
Shake, Shake out of me
All that is carnal.

— Shaker song, ca. 1835[1]

When he was a boy, Henry Blinn must have been one of those maddening children who only seem to know one word: "Why?" He appears to have been a seeker, and a questioner, from his childhood. The regular answers weren't good enough for him, and he kept on asking questions. He must have driven his mother crazy.

Henry Clay Blinn was born in 1824, a peaceful and productive time for the young United States. The recent wars with Britain were over, the Industrial Revolution was humming; America was rich with fertile acres, ripe with possibilities. Henry came from a seafaring family, and his mother made her home in the port city of Providence, Rhode Island, with her many children, of whom Henry was the youngest. His father had died at sea when Henry was an infant.

Like many adolescents, Henry felt a drive to seek out something, although he wasn't sure what. He had no interest in following his father's trade and going to sea. His parents were not members of any church, but at an early age he was already searching for some sort of spiritual home. It's a rare ten-year-old who is eager for religious improvement, but he was joyful at being "permitted" to attend divine service and Sunday School.[2]

Henry longed to get an education, but money was tight in the Blinn house after the untimely death of his father, and Henry did not have the luxury of much schooling, or any choice of careers. His working life began at the age of twelve, when he was hired as an errand boy. Later he was apprenticed to a merchant, his days spent tending the fire and sweeping out the shop.

But he knew that there was something else, something more, waiting for him. At fourteen, he recalled, "I began to grow uneasy in regard to my place of business and was so discontented that it became a matter of investigation." He attributed what came next to the guidance of "a holy light."[3]

By chance, one Sunday afternoon, "I observed a man passing so quietly on the street and being dressed so differently from the other citizens that he attracted my attention, and at the same time awakened in my mind an interest to know who he was and where he lived. I saw the man a second time, and soon after learned that he was a Shaker." The sight of that oddly-dressed stranger had a powerful influence on Henry, but the word "Shaker" conveyed nothing to him. "It then became a puzzle to know what a Shaker was."[4]

Henry was not the only one who was puzzled. "No one could give any information where he lived or concerning his religious belief. It was thought very singular that I should be attracted toward a stranger, and why I was I could not tell. I only knew this, that his general appearance pleased me, and I would like very much to live with him."[5]

Soon there was a report of another Shaker passing through town, and Henry immediately paid him a visit. The Shaker, one Nathan Willard, must have observed that here was a promising convert. He assured young Henry that the Shakers were "a very kind and charitable people . . . willing to receive good boys and girls." After one conversation, Henry "became fully determined to accompany him to his home."[6]

Henry's family, like the families of many Shaker converts before and since, were baffled, suspicious, and finally, appalled. They "protested against the wild scheme of going among the mountains of New Hampshire," but their pleas fell on deaf ears. Henry was certain that this was the path for him.[7]

The idealistic fourteen-year-old abruptly quit his job, made "hurried farewells," and left his family, friends, and home town behind. He was headed into an unfamiliar landscape of dark pine forests and granite hills. "It was the journey of a young Pilgrim," he proudly recorded when he wrote his autobiography many decades later. He claimed that he never regretted his choice.[8]

His pilgrimage was a hundred and twenty miles, by rail, stagecoach, and wagon — a considerable distance in those days when folk frequently lived their entire lives, died, and were buried in the same little town they were born in. Years later, he vividly recalled the first view of his new home (Figure 2). As he approached Canterbury after the long journey, the Shaker village stood outlined against the autumn evening sky, a cluster of "white and light yellow houses with bright red roofs . . . a beautiful picture on the mind."[9] He made his home on the beautiful hilltop for the next sixty-seven years.

❧

Figure 2. Henry Blinn recalled that his first view of Canterbury Shaker Village was "a beautiful picture on the mind." Use courtesy of Shaker Museum and Library, Old Chatham and New Lebanon, NY.

"It was a Sabbath morning . . . very quiet,"[10] when his entry was recorded: "Henry Clay Blinn, September 9, 1838," sandwiched in between Harriet Burns, who was "received" on September 5, and William Maloon, John Ingalls, and Hyla Peacock, who all arrived that same autumn.[11] "I was among a new class of people, whose language, dress and manners were so unlike those of the city; yet their kindness found access to my heart."[12] It seems that young Henry felt, right away, that he had come home.

His new family dressed plainly. Brothers generally wore dark breeches, vests, and jackets, topped off by flat straw hats. Their hair was often cropped in an unusual cut, long in back, with short, straight bangs across the forehead. Sisters wore simple dresses, devoid of frills and furbelows, though colors were not forbidden. Over their shoulders they wore a scarf or a short cape that modestly covered the bosom. A white cap that hid the hair was a sign that the wearer had signed a binding agreement called the Covenant, and was a full-fledged Shaker.

On Henry's first day in the village, he attended a "meeting." A Shaker worship service was a strange experience indeed, as Henry recorded long after.

"The marching, singing and speaking were quite unlike anything that I had ever seen or heard," he wrote, with his usual understatement.[13] "Visions, singing new hymns, the personating of those who had passed into the spirit land, and bowing and bending and shaking."[14]

Many Shakers unquestioningly accepted the appearance of spiritual visitors. Celestial voices were often reported during services, speaking from the spirits of departed souls ranging from Jesus Christ to Pocahontas. A Massachusetts Shaker wrote matter-of-factly in his journal: "In the evening many of the ancients attended our meeting, such as Noah, Abraham, Jeremiah, and Isaiah, also some of the ancient sisters, the Virgin Mary and others."[15] Shaker services were intense experiences. "We have a very good meeting," the anonymous journalist commented. "In meeting about twenty-two hours."[16]

So it wasn't much like Sunday School back in Providence, Rhode Island. Shakers worshipped as "souls, laboring under the power of God, and roaring like *the sound of many waters* . . . shaking and trembling; prophesying or speaking with new tongues; singing and dancing; leaping and shouting . . . with such various supernatural effects of the power of God, as appeared to the blind spectators of this world like the most unaccountable confusion."[17] It might have been enough to frighten a less adventurous Pilgrim.

But Henry stuck it out, and soon began to learn the ropes. As that first autumn progressed, he began to unravel the puzzle of "what a Shaker was."

He found that to be a Shaker, it was necessary to be a hard worker. A deacon promptly set the boy to sawing staves to make pails; he had a good deal of sawing to do, as the village "made about 1,000 pails a year for sale."[18] The Shakers kept Henry even busier than his old master had, back home. But in addition to labor for the body, there was work for the mind as well. These kind people had strange beliefs, and perplexing new ideas.

The stumbling block for many converts, of course, was the Shakers' total commitment to celibacy. Henry never recorded if, or how, he struggled with this unbending requirement of Shakerism. But once he signed the Covenant, he willingly resigned himself to a lifetime of chastity.

The Shakers had other ideas, too, highly unorthodox for their time. For instance, they believed that African-Americans and Native Americans were human beings, who might be considered Brothers and Sisters. In the World, women could not vote, but Shaker women exercised powerful positions of leadership.

Another quirk of the Shakers, Henry found, was their dedication to non-violence. Even corporal punishment for children was rare. Although his lack of schooling put him far behind the other students, in the Shaker classroom Henry was never thrashed into learning. It was "contrary to order" even to abuse an animal. The Believers had been staunch pacifists from their beginnings — they had refused to participate in the American Revolution and the War of 1812. Shakers taught the young Henry that war was one of the World's greatest evils.

Perhaps the most astounding thing of all about the Shakers, Henry discovered, was that they referred to themselves as the Believers in the Second Appearing of Christ. At first glance, this had not seemed unusual — many people in the early nineteenth century were eagerly awaiting Jesus' Second Coming, and prophesying doom and the end of the world when Christ came again. But the Shakers were certain that the Second Appearing had *already* occurred — quite recently. And it had taken place in a manner that few would have expected. In an era when women were viewed as the inferior sex, denied many of the most basic rights, the Shakers worshipped a male-female duality. They believed that the second appearance of Christ's spirit had been manifested in a woman.

"The foundation pillars of the church of Christ — the two anointed ones . . . between whom the covenant of eternal life is established," Shakers believed, were two people — "the man who is called JESUS, and the woman who is called MOTHER."[19]

Notes

[1] Patterson, Daniel. *The Shaker Spiritual*. Mineola, NY: Dover Publications, Inc., 2000, p. 254. This lively dancing song was made by Elder Issachar Bates.

[2] *In Memoriam: Henry C. Blinn, 1824–1905*. Concord, NH: Rumford Printing Co., 1905, p. 6.

[3] Ibid., p. 11.

[4] Ibid., p. 12.

[5] Ibid.

[6] Ibid., p. 13.

[7] Ibid.

[8] Ibid.

[9] Ibid., p. 14.

[10] Ibid., p. 15.

[11] Blinn, *Record*, vol. 2, p. 261.

[12] Blinn, *Memoriam*, p. 14.

[13] Ibid., p. 15.

[14] Ibid., p. 27.

[15] Sears, Clara Endicott. *Gleanings from Shaker Journals*. Boston, MA: Houghton Mifflin Co., 1916, p. 225.

[16] Ibid.

[17] Youngs, Benjamin S., and Calvin Green. *Testimony of Christ's Second Appearing*. Albany, NY: Van Benthuysen, Printer, 1856, p. 629.

[18] Blinn, *Memoriam*, p. 15.

[19] Youngs and Green. *Testimony of Christ's Second Appearing*. p. 384.

This Blessed Fire

At Manchester, in England, this blessed fire began,
And like a flame in stubble, from house to house it ran:
A few at first receiv'd it, and did their lusts forsake;
And soon their inward power brought on a mighty shake.

— "Mother Ann's Song"[1]

Many of those who met Ann Lee, looked into her piercing blue eyes, or heard her powerful voice raised in song remembered her vividly decades after her death. Henry Blinn, like all Shaker youngsters, must often have listened to exciting tales of Mother Ann and her adventures. Henry might have heard some of these stories first-hand from elderly Brothers and Sisters who had known her in life and still cherished their memories of this remarkable woman. Ann Lee was illiterate, and like Jesus, she left no written words behind, but her pithy remarks and the stories of her wondrous doings were passed from Shaker to Shaker.

There are no photographs or portraits of Ann Lee. She was described as "rather exceeding the ordinary size of women," and she had chestnut brown hair and blue eyes.[2] She was a middle-aged former textile worker, probably a bit stout and heavy-bodied after four pregnancies, and her hands must have been roughened after a lifetime of hard work. She sounds an unlikely figure to forge a new religion.

But Ann Lee surely had a towering personality. All her life, few remained neutral towards this determined woman. People wanted to kneel down and worship her as a God — or murder her.

Perhaps the closest we can come to a feeling for her physical presence is a rocking chair preserved in the Fruitlands Museum in Massachusetts, which according to tradition is "Mother Ann's chair." The old chair is short-legged and plain, solidly built. Strong, thick arms thrust forward like clenched fists. Like the religion Ann Lee brought to the New World, it has lasted a long time.

Ann Lee was born in Manchester, England, on February 29, 1736, a date that was for many years celebrated by the Shakers with song and feasting. Her birth fell on a strange date, which doesn't exist three years out of four — the "leap day" in a leap year, a time when, by tradition, women can speak up and propose to men. This makes her birth-date appropriate indeed, for Ann was nothing if not outspoken.

She was the second child of John Lee, a blacksmith, and his wife, a shadowy figure of whom almost nothing is known, not even her name. Six other siblings followed Ann in rapid succession. Her parents and their eight children must have been a tight fit in the few rooms of their small house in Toad Lane. Manchester in the early eighteenth century was not yet in the grip of the Industrial Revolution that would shortly fill it with smoke-belching factories; some green fields and cow pastures remained, and a broad river ran nearby. Young Ann, however, had little time to play in the meadows and explore the riverbanks. Ann Lee often extolled the virtues of hard work, and she practiced what she later preached. She began a career as a textile worker, probably at a very young age. In those days, children of kindergarten age regularly worked to help support the family, and schooling was a luxury that would have been difficult to afford for a blacksmith with eight children. Ann prepared cotton for looms, cut velvet for hats, and later, worked as a cook. Her days flowed on, undoubtedly filled with hard work, and uneventful as far as we know, until the day when Ann Lee, now in her early twenties, attended a very unusual religious service. After that day, nothing would ever be the same for her again.

❧

Two newcomers — James and Jane Wardley — had recently arrived in Manchester. Little is known about this unusual couple, who were married but lived as brother and sister in a celibate relationship. Former Quakers, they had broken away from that group a few years previously.

The Quakers, dating from the 1600s, were by this time a well-known sect. Their nickname came from the fact that in their early days they sometimes "quaked" at the word of the Lord, but Quaker meetings in this era were generally restrained and introspective. The Wardleys' style of worship was wildly different from Quakerism, and also from the official Church of England routine.

Henry the Eighth's revolutionary brand of Protestantism was two hundred years old by this time, and had long since ceased to be controversial. England's mainstream religion had settled into a sedate pattern, in which the congregation sang a decorous hymn or two, then settled down to doze through a long, improving sermon. The Wardleys, however, conducted religious services in which worshippers were not passive observers, but energetic participants.

When these odd Believers felt the Holy Spirit descend on them, they would not only quake, but roll on the floor, shout, leap, and spin around like tops till they fell, exhausted. Their exhibitions struck observers as sheer lunacy. "They were affected, under the power of God, with a mighty shaking; and were occasionally exercised in singing, shouting, or walking the floor . . . shoving each other about . . . or swiftly passing and repassing each other, like clouds agitated by a mighty wind."[3]

An unconventional church service, to be sure. But what most observers failed to understand was the utter conviction of the participants that they were in direct contact with God, and that it was the Holy Sprit, and no human will, that made them tremble and spin. Ann Lee must have been profoundly moved by the experience. She joined the group in 1758.[4]

The bizarre goings-on of this small group did not sit well with the townsfolk. The noise of the services was frequently complained of. A story in an English newspaper described the worshippers as "trembling, shaking, and screeching in the most dreadful manner . . . they disturb the whole neighborhood for some considerable distance, and continue sometimes whole nights in the most shocking distortions and commotions."[5] The citizens of Manchester began to lose patience — and grow suspicious.

The early eighteenth century was a time of religious upheaval in Europe, with many groups splintering off from established religions. Dissidents were not regarded as harmless eccentrics, as we might regard, say, the Amish, or Hare Krishnas, today. These new sects were viewed as dangerously subversive, a threat to the established order; people feared them, seeing them as more al Quaida than Amish. The Wardleys' group was eyed with fear, scorn, and a complete lack of understanding. The townsfolk derisively called them the "Shaking Quakers," or simply "the Shakers."

~

The next major event in Ann Lee's life, recorded in the parish records, was her marriage in 1762 to one Abraham Stanley (or Standerin), a blacksmith like her father. Her name is written on the wedding certificate, still preserved in Manchester cathedral; next to the clerk's neat script, Ann made her mark — a big, forceful "x" that goes outside the lines. Just above is her new husband's mark — he, also illiterate, made a small, tidy "x" on the document.[6]

In the early days of their marriage, it probably seemed as though they would be an ordinary couple, living out their lives in the town where they were born. Soon the young couple was expecting a baby. The child was born but, as so often happened in those days, died in infancy. They tried again, but their next child died as well. Another birth — and another tragedy. And another. Ann Lee experienced, one by one, the deaths of four children. Only one is recorded in the church records: Elizabeth, born in 1764, and died in 1766.

To bury a child is perhaps the most devastating thing that can happen to a woman: the tiny form in the tiny coffin; the little face that should be alive with laughter, stilled and marble cold. It surely left its mark on Ann's face. It left indelible marks on her mind as well. She had what we might call today a nervous breakdown.

Long after her death, her followers wrote down their recollections of her in a book called *Testimonies of Mother Ann*.[7] With awe, they recalled her "watchings, fastings, tears, and incessant cries to God."[8] "Sometimes, for whole nights together, her cries, screeches and groans were such as to fill every soul around her with fear and trembling." The Shakers saw many parallels between Ann's experience and that of Jesus, and recorded that "she was often in such extreme agony of soul as caused the blood to perspire through the pores of her skin." Ann endured years of this intense suffering, and "her flesh wasted away till she became like a mere skeleton."[9]

Finally, she came to some kind of terms with her grief and her religious convictions. Ann Lee had a revelation. "The light and power of God [was] revealed in Ann," wrote a Shaker, long after.[10] "I saw," Ann said simply, "and knew what I saw."[11]

Her certainty must have been utterly convincing. The Wardleys promptly yielded leadership of the group to her, and she was acknowledged as the "first spiritual Mother in Christ, and the second heir of the covenant of life in the new creation."[12] From this time forth, the bereaved and childless woman was known as "Mother Ann."

❧

At some time after the deaths of her four children, Ann turned away from sex for good. She insisted that celibacy was the essential path to redemption, and was adamant that "the lustful gratifications of the flesh" were the "source and foundation of human corruption."[13] She had grim warnings for sinners. "I now see, in open vision, souls in hell, under torment for their sins, committed though lust…They are bound in the prisons of hell, and their torment appears like melted lead, poured through them, in the same parts where they have taken their carnal pleasure."[14]

The writers of the *Testimonies* recalled her story that, "in early youth, she had a great abhorrence of the fleshly cohabitation of the sexes; and so great was her sense of its impurity, that she often admonished her mother against it; which coming to her father's ears, he threatened and actually attempted to whip her; upon which she threw herself into her mother's arms and clung round her to escape his strokes."[15]

Perhaps Ann's abhorrence of "fleshly cohabitation" was born when she saw her mother struggling through repeated pregnancies, exhausted by constant childbearing, and possibly even dying of childbirth — the cause of her mother's death is not known, but childbirth was then, as it had been for millennia, a leading cause of death for women. Her extreme aversion to sex may have been a reflection of some deeper trauma of childhood abuse or molestation. Or perhaps the devastating losses of her infants made her determined never to face that situation again. At any rate, she insisted on total celibacy for all her adherents.

In spite of the fact that they were forbidden to "wallow in the filth of sexuality," the Shakers were increasing in number.[16] Ann's charisma and forceful conviction won convert after convert, till the size of the group grew to sixty or more. But as the number of Shakers rose, so did tensions in Manchester. The citizens were out of patience with this group of eccentrics who screamed and shook and disturbed the peace. As the Shakers put it, "the powerful operations of the spirit of God, which prevailed in the meetings . . . stirred up the rage and enmity" of all.[17] The Shakers were mocked, jailed, and assaulted with increasing frequency.

One of Ann Lee's closest disciples was a young man named James Whittaker. On a journey one day, he sat down to rest by the side of the road, and, as often happened with the Shakers, a celestial vision obtruded itself on his everyday life. "While I was sitting there, I saw a vision of America, and I saw a large tree, and every leaf thereof shone with such brightness, as made it appear like a burning torch, representing the Church of Christ, which will yet be established in this land."[18] The Shakers often took dreams and visions very seriously. In 1774, Mother Ann announced that the Shakers were leaving for America.

This was a leap of faith indeed. Out of more than sixty Shakers, only eight were willing to leave their familiar surroundings and go off to a wilderness filled with dangerous beasts and savage Indians. The American colonies were also seething with political unrest that was about to develop into a full-blown revolution.

But the loyal eight packed up their belongings. Ann must have made a considerable impact on the men of her own family, because not only her husband, but her brother came, too. Ann's husband eventually left her, but her brother William remained faithful to the end of his life. The fifty or so remaining Shakers, bereft of Ann's charismatic presence, fell away from the faith and Shakerism died out completely in England. But the infant religion was soon on its way to the New World, in an old and leaky craft called the *Mariah*.

The Shakers soon began their usual worship, lurching back and forth on the heaving deck, and singing loudly. The crew threatened to throw their strange passengers over the side if they didn't stop the noise. Again tensions rose, but divine providence, or luck, took a hand. During a storm, the *Mariah* sprang a leak so wide that the sailors were unable to pump out the water. As the ship began to founder, Mother Ann rose to the occasion.

"Be of good cheer," she reassured the captain. "There shall not a hair of our heads perish; we shall all arrive safe to America. I was just now sitting by the mast, and I saw a bright angel of God, through whom I received this promise."[19]

The sailors and the Shakers then joined forces to pump out the rising water, and the day was saved. This exciting event must have been an oft-told story in later years, and is perhaps the first and best example of Mother Ann's most famous precept: "Put your hands to work, and give your hearts to God."[20] The combination of unwavering faith in the Almighty, aided by energetic hard work, would become the hallmark of the Shakers.

They landed safely in New York City on August 6, 1774, a date that was celebrated by Shakers ever after. The newcomers disembarked, doubtless happy to be on solid ground at last, and walked along a wide road known as the Broad Way. Two centuries ago,

Manhattan was a rural place; New Yorkers sat outside on their porches to escape the heat of the day, which must have seemed oppressive to folk used to the cool climate of England. Mother Ann plainly had a knack for discerning those who would be open to her teaching; she began a conversation with a woman who eventually invited Ann into her home, and gave her a job as a laundress.

The other Shakers did menial work as well, until they had earned enough money to purchase a tract of wild swampland near Albany, New York, called "Niskeyuna" by the Native Americans. In the spring of 1776, Mother Ann and her little flock left the city and sailed up the broad Hudson River. As usual, this was faith and practicality blended. It was a symbolic "going into the wilderness," seeking the shining tree of Brother James's dream. And it was also an excellent time for the Shakers to beat a strategic retreat. A war was starting.

❧

The Shakers, right from the beginning, wanted to distance themselves from the World's affairs — especially its wars. The American Revolution was heating up — a British man-o'war was patrolling the waters around Manhattan, and the Shakers heard gunfire as the British fired at the city and the American militia replied. The wild lands of Niskeyuna must have seemed a welcome refuge from a city that was just about to be invaded by thirty thousand British soldiers.

The forests and wetlands of upstate New York were "unimproved" land, which seemed to these urban folk, as James Whittaker put it, "pretty much waste."[21] However, the land's original inhabitants would have disagreed with that description. The Mohawks, the easternmost nation of the Iroquois confederation, were already farming the fertile land — "Niskeyuna" is from an Iroquois word meaning "corn flats." Most of the European settlers who had been battling the wilderness regarded the Native Americans with fear and suspicion. But the Shakers had an affinity for their new neighbors; perhaps they saw them as fellow outcasts. And the Mohawks seemed to feel a sort of spiritual connection with Mother Ann, referring to her as "the good woman."[22]

Instead of regarding the Native Americans as savages, the Shakers appreciated their knowledge of the land and its raw materials. Ann's brother William is described as speaking to the Indians in their native tongue. The Shakers, then and later, were willing to learn from other cultures. In particular, they absorbed two Native American skills that would become classically "Shaker": the knowledge of the medicinal herbs that grew in fields and woods, and the ability to weave baskets of beauty and practicality combined.

The Shakers built log cabins, farmed the land, and laid up supplies of food for the Believers who, Mother Ann assured them, would soon come flocking "like doves."[23] And indeed, converts began to arrive. These were turbulent times in the young nation; as well as the political revolution, many Americans were experiencing a religious upheaval, so that revival meetings, apocalyptic prophets, and would-be Messiahs abounded. Religious groups such as the New Light ministry in Massachusetts began to hear of the dancing Shakers and their female leader, the "Elect Lady." Many came to investigate, and stayed to join.

But the Shakers were still foreigners in America, with inexplicable notions about not fighting the invading Redcoats. Their neighbors eyed them with increasing suspicion. The government of New York State had established a commission for "detecting and defeating Conspiracies," and the commissioners stated that the "set of people who call themselves shaking Quakers . . . [are] highly pernicious and of destructive tendency to the Freedom & Independence of the United States of America." Shakers were accused of disturbing the peace and "daily dissuading the friends to the American cause from taking up Arms in defense of their Liberties."[24] They were suspected of spying, and of supplying the enemy with livestock and food supplies. Several Shakers, including Ann Lee, were imprisoned.

Finally the anti-British hysteria began to subside, as the Revolutionary War drew toward its close. Ann's loyal followers were successful in obtaining bail, and she was eventually released. She returned to Niskeyuna, but did not stay there long. Like Jesus, after a period of reflection in the wilderness, she set out on a journey to preach, heal, and seek converts.

Her journey lasted more than two years, as she crossed and re-crossed upstate New York, Massachusetts, and Connecticut. Several Shaker leaders went with her, and at the services they conducted, many converts were made. Ann's intense gaze, her remarkable singing, and her personal magnetism were compelling. She seemed to have an almost uncanny ability to ferret out people's innermost troubles and secrets. Many people accepted that she was divinely inspired.

Others who heard her, however, were roused to a fury that erupted in surprising violence against this seemingly harmless group, whose only crime was their eccentricity. The Shakers' unorthodox worship techniques roused ire, but there were issues that were even more threatening than all that singing and dancing.

Ann Lee ignored the conventions of family and society. She preached the most radical words of Jesus. "If any man come to me, and hate not his father, and mother, and wife, and children, and brethren, and sisters, yea, and his own life also, he cannot be my disciple."[25] Converts sometimes abandoned their spouses or their children to join the strange sect. Bitter relatives frequently headed the angry mobs who hurled stones and dung, beat Shakers with horse-whips, or threatened to burn their dwellings over their heads.

Ann was often seen by the Shakers as the female parallel to Jesus, but she did not endure her revilers with Christ-like meekness. On one occasion, when she was being questioned about a variety of trumped-up charges, she lost her temper with her inquisitor, a Colonel David Wells.

"'Is it not a shame for you . . . to come here, at the head of a mob . . . to persecute an innocent people?'" she demanded.

Her accuser, "stung with this reproof, replied . . . 'If you don't hold your tongue, I'll cane you.'

"'Do you pretend to be a gentleman,' [said Mother,] 'and are going to cane a poor weak woman! What a shame it is!'" One can imagine the resolute woman, hands on her hips, blue eyes blazing as she faced down her attackers.[26]

Things didn't get better. Though the traveling Shakers succeeded in attracting devout converts, the inhabitants of almost every town they came to were hostile. Shakers were repeatedly insulted and abused. In Massachusetts, James Whittaker and other Brothers were brutally flogged. The violence rose to a crescendo when Ann herself was kidnapped from the house where she was staying. Dragged downstairs by her heels, she was assaulted by a mob; the clothes were torn off her back as the ruffians attempted to ascertain if she was indeed a woman.

Ann Lee returned to Niskeyuna in 1783, having made hundreds of converts. She must have been worn out by her travels and the physical abuse she had received, for she died less than a year later. There was no overt cause of her quiet passing. The woman who had shaken and sung during her religious observances slipped away "without a struggle or a groan."[27] She was forty-eight years old.

∞

The pattern has recurred throughout history — a unique individual starts a revolution, or a religion, based at least in part on their own dazzling personality: Jesus, Buddha, Mohammed, Mahatma Gandhi, Mother Ann . . . but when the charismatic leader is gone, what do the survivors do? What happens to the everyday mortals, the ordinary folk — the people like you and me — who are left behind? Like Peter and the other bewildered apostles, Mother Ann's successors were faced with the daunting task of keeping an infant religion alive in a very unfriendly environment. They had to consider a host of threats, pitfalls, and options; there were a thousand possible pathways for the Believers to take.

Like Jesus, Mother Ann left no written set of instructions for developing a new religion. But she had prophesied that "Souls will embrace it [the gospel] by hundreds and by thousands,"[28] and her words were coming true. By the time of her death there were hundreds of Shakers scattered across a wide geographic area. There were countless practical difficulties for them to solve: how to obtain food, clothing, shelter. And foremost in their thoughts was the all-important food of the soul — how to nurture the spiritual life.

Perhaps some of the Shakers were, deep down, a little uncomfortable with the sensual passion of the original worship style, as unbridled as a pagan rite of spring. The Shaker leaders began to root their unconventional religion in a firm soil of hard-headed New England practicality. They had the tough job of trying to systematize a wildly individual, emotional religion; they sought to organize ecstasy.

But the Shakers were never afraid of hard work. Their religion was their first priority, but they focused on neither the promise of a blissful afterlife nor the doom-and-gloom of Judgment Day. Instead, they chose an ambitious mission — to create a way of life here and now, on Earth, that would be a mirror of the perfect heaven above.

Notes

[1] Cohen, Joel, editor. *Simple Gifts: Shaker Chants and Spirituals*. A Recording of Shaker Music by the Shakers of Sabbathday Lake and the Boston Camerata. 1 Audio CD, Erato Disques, 1995. Liner notes written by Sister Frances Carr and Joel Cohen, p. 24. "Mother Ann's Song" is a ballad that tells the story of the Shakers' history. It was often sung on August 6th, the anniversary of Mother Ann's arrival in the New World.

[2] *Testimonies*, p. 343.

[3] Francis, Richard. *Ann the Word*. New York, NY: Arcade Publishing, 2001, p. 25.

[4] Mrs. Wardley had high status as leader of the group along with her husband, and was known as "Mother Jane." The Wardleys may have been aware of, and influenced by, a group known as the French Prophets, or Camisards, some of whom fled France in the early 1700s, settled in England, and attracted considerable attention. The Camisards also practiced a form of worship that involved agitated, dance-like movements, and they revered several female leaders and prophets. The Wardleys' "new" religion obviously drew much from the Quakers, notably their belief in non-violence and pacifism. Shakerism may also have drawn from John and Charles Wesley's Methodism, and from George Whitefield, an impassioned preacher and evangelical Anglican.

[5] Morse, Flo. *Shakers and the World's People.* New York, NY: Dodd, Mead, and Co., 1980, p. 3.

[6] Reproduced in Morse, *Shakers and the World's People,* p. 12.

[7] In 1816, the Shakers compiled a book entitled *Testimonies of the Life, Character, Revelations and Doctrines of Our Ever Blessed Mother Ann Lee, and the Elders with Her; through whom the Word of Eternal Life was Opened in this Day of Christ's Second Appearing: Collected from Living Witnesses, by Order of the Ministry, in Union with the Church.* The stories in it were memories of Mother Ann which had been recounted orally, and only written down many years after the events occurred. As Stephen J. Stein in his classic *The Shaker Experience in America* notes, "these accounts must be used with great caution" (Stein, *Shaker Experience,* p. 28). Shortly after its release, *Testimonies* was withdrawn from circulation by the Shaker leadership. It was not published in "the World" and even rank-and-file Shakers were not allowed to see it; it was made available only to the highest levels of the church. Perhaps the Elders feared that a too-candid portrait of the tempestuous and outspoken Mother Ann, warts and all, might discourage the faithful. It became known as "The Secret Book of the Elders."

Richard Francis points out in *Ann the Word* that "the fact that the book proved such a hot potato when it was first published suggests that the material had not been extensively sanitized and adapted" (Francis, *Ann the Word,* p. 360). In any case, it is the main source for anecdotes of Mother Ann's eventful and dramatic life.

An abridged version, which took out many earthy and fascinating details, was published by the Shakers in the more sedate Victorian days of 1888, and made widely available.

[8] *Testimonies,* p. 4.

[9] Ibid., p. 5.

[10] Ibid., p. 7.

[11] Ibid., p. 48.

[12] Ibid., p. 7.

[13] Ibid., p. 6.

[14] Ibid., p. 304.

[15] Ibid., p. 3.

[16] Evans, Frederick William. *Autobiography of a Shaker, and Revelation of the Apocalypse.* New York, NY: American News Co., 1888, p. 179.

[17] *Testimonies,* p. 7.

[18] Ibid., p. 66.

[19] Ibid., p. 68.

[20] Ibid., p. 346.

[21] Patterson, *Shaker Spiritual,* p. 68.

[22] *Testimonies,* p. 202.

[23] Ibid., p. 14.

[24] Stein, *Shaker Experience*, p. 14.

[25] *Holy Bible*, Luke 14:26.

[26] *Testimonies*, p. 143.

[27] Ibid., p. 351.

[28] Ibid., p. 216.

Millennial Laws

Yea we will rejoice with freedom
In this straight little narrow way
Here is the fold and the lambs all feeding
On this green we'll skip and play.

— Shaker song, ca. 1830[1]

The Shaker Elders of the Central Ministry were concerned about an issue that had been causing heated argument among the Brethren of many villages. In 1875, after lengthy debate and due deliberation, the Elders, who had the last word on Shaker doctrines, issued a "Circular Epistle" discussing the pros and cons of a contentious issue, "the agitated subject of beard wearing."[2]

The Elders decreed that Brothers should "wear such portion of the beard as the shirt collar would principally cover, clipping it short with shears," and recommended that beard-wearers should have "the whiskers closely trimmed & the beard below the chin, and would recommend to confine this to from three to four inches in length." In a final note, they cautioned that "A moustache should not be worn, petted, curled & twisted, for the sake of pride & worldly fashion."[3]

Today, we read this document with a smile and a shake of the head. Why would anyone concern themselves so greatly over such monumental trivia? And who would willingly give up their freedom, we wonder, to live such a controlled and ordered life? Surely no one would want to live in a society that had such absurd rules, with censorious Elders measuring the length of beards and keeping a sharp look-out for any surreptitious mustache-twirling. Why on earth would an intelligent, rebellious adolescent like Henry Blinn — why would anyone — join such a group of nit-pickers?

Few would linger in such a society unless they found there something deeper, unless there were glorious possibilities to "rejoice with freedom" in what appeared on the surface to be an irritatingly "straight little narrow way." Henry was able to look beneath the surface, and he found that where the water is narrow, there can be a powerful current.

Even after the death of Mother Ann, the Shakers continued to break rules as well as make them. After the untimely death of her right-hand man James Whittaker at the age of thirty-six, the leadership passed out of the hands of the original English disciples. The reins were taken by Joseph Meacham, one of the first American-born converts to Shakerism and a favorite of Mother Ann, who prophesied: "Joseph Meacham is my first born son in America. He will gather the Church in order; but I shall not live to see it."[4] As Ann perhaps saw, he was a remarkably unconventional man. When he became the acknowledged leader of the Shakers, Joseph Meacham did an extraordinary thing — he chose to divide his power with another person. Most remarkably of all, that person was a woman.

Even the Shakers were taken aback by this outrageous step. "It was such a new thing and so unexpected that there was something of a labor before the matter was finished," one astonished Shaker commented.[5] Meacham braved the controversy and insisted that Lucy Wright, another beloved disciple of Mother Ann, was the person to work with him to guide the Shakers into the new century. After Meacham's startling decision, the Shaker leadership was divided between male and female, with pairs of Elders and Eldresses working together. From that time on, Shaker women had a vastly greater level of inclusion in decision-making than did women in the outside World. The Shakers had one of the first organizational structures in Anglo-American society that gave women formal offices with titles and defined powers, and allowed them to serve alongside male leaders. Meacham and Wright set the example for future Shakers: man and woman working side by side.

∾

As the Shakers were getting themselves organized, the Revolutionary War was just ending. America was a brash young country pulling itself up by its bootstraps. The brand new republic was fertile ground for social experimentation, and America's promise of religious toleration lured many dissident groups from the Old World. A long list of Utopian and/or religious communities — such as the True Inspirationists, the Harmonists, the Owenites, and the Perfectionists — established themselves in America in the 1800s.

It was an era when many were fervently seeking religious truths, and perhaps America seemed like a land where anything was possible. When a group known as the Millerites predicted that Christ would come again on October 22, 1844, tens of thousands awaited the event with joyful expectation. After that day, known as the "Great Disappointment," many irate Millerites joined the Shakers.[6]

As with the Shakers, it was a community's sexual mores that drew the most criticism. The Perfectionists outraged convention with their belief in "complex marriage," a form of polygamy in which adult males and females considered themselves "married" to the group and not to a single partner.

Some of these organizations were religious, some secular; some were celibate, some were decidedly not. They were dedicated to many of the same ideals as the Shakers, with convictions that were doubtless as sincere. But all of them struggled with the harsh realities of putting food on the table. One instructive example is the group of Transcendentalists who settled at a pleasant farm in Massachusetts that they called Fruitlands.

These optimistic Utopians were led by Bronson Alcott — accompanied by his family, including his daughter, Louisa May — and a radical thinker named Charles Lane. Ralph Waldo Emerson, observing them with interest, remarked that, although Lane's intentions were noble, his "hands were indeed too far from his head."[7] "They look well in July," Emerson observed drily. "We will see them in December."[8]

The founding members of Fruitlands lacked even the most basic of farming skills, and were "so busy discussing and defining great duties that they forgot to perform the small ones."[9] Lane and Bronson Alcott often played hookey from chores to spend the day with the Shakers at nearby Harvard Village, whose success they sought to emulate. But at Fruitlands the philosophers scorned the use of animal labor to pull plows because they did not want to "subjugate" the oxen. "Manure was not allowed to profane the virgin soil," but without fertilizer, the harvest was small indeed.[10] The society collapsed after six months.

The Shakers' hands were never too far from their heads. James Whittaker, Joseph Meacham, Lucy Wright, and other Shaker leaders never forgot Ann Lee's oft-repeated maxim: "Hands to work, hearts to God." They created a practical, organized way of living that could sustain their religion. To this day, the Shakers are the longest lasting religious communal group in America, with a record of more than two centuries.

In Mother Ann's time, many Shakers had remained in their homes, among family members and neighbors who were non-Shakers. Converts attempted to interact with "the World" while holding fast to their principles, as Quakers do today. But "bearing the full cross" of Shakerism, including celibacy, was all but impossible while caught up in the mainstream of the World's affairs. Meacham and Wright continued the process, begun by James Whittaker, of leading the Shakers on a course of withdrawal from the World.

The loose clusters of Shakers were gathered into communities, often centered on the nucleus of a farm belonging to an entire family who had converted. Others would move in, bringing their tools and furniture. Neighboring tracts of land were bought. At the close of the eighteenth century, Shaker communities were formed, one after the other. The original Niskeyuna settlement, now called Watervliet, was replaced as the hub of Shaker activities by New Lebanon, near the New York-Massachusetts border. Mother Ann's missionary journey had made devout converts in Massachusetts, and Shakers gathered at Hancock, Harvard, Tyringham, and Shirley. Two communities — one in Connecticut, one in New Hampshire — were named Enfield. Benjamin Whitcher, in 1792, donated a tract of fertile land in New Hampshire upon which Canterbury Shaker Village still stands today. And Shakerism spread north, to Alfred and Sabbathday Lake in Maine. By 1800 there were eleven fledgling Shaker communities in New York and New England (Figure 3). Later, each village was given a spiritual name: Hancock became the "City of Peace," New Lebanon was called "Holy Mount," Shirley was "Pleasant Garden." Canterbury was known as "Holy Ground."

Mother Ann had prophesied that "the next opening of the gospel will be in the south-west; it will be at a great distance, and there will be a great work of God."[11] She added that she herself would not live to see it. After her death, the Shakers remembered

Early Shaker Communities

1. Niskeyuna / Watervliet, NY
2. New Lebanon, NY
3. Tyringham, MA
4. Hancock, MA
5. Harvard, MA
6. Shirley, MA
7. Enfield, CT
8. Canterbury, NH
9. Enfield, NH
10. Alfred, ME
11. Sabbathday, ME

Figure 3. By the beginning of the nineteenth century, eleven Shaker communities had been established in New York and New England.

this prediction, and set out to make it come true. Missionaries were dispatched into the wilderness, braving Indian territory. Some Shaker Brothers traveled more than a thousand miles — on foot! — to seek converts in the frontier lands. Pleasant Hill was established in the wilds of Kentucky in 1806, three years before Abraham Lincoln was born in a log cabin about seventy-five miles away.

Other communities formed, in Ohio, Indiana, and Kentucky. More and more Shaker villages filled with enthusiastic converts. The souls were flocking like doves, indeed.

When a person left his or her home to join a Shaker village, the biological families left behind were stunned, bewildered, or in some cases, fighting mad. The Shakers were involved in some spectacular — and very well-publicized — divorce cases. Sometimes the converted parent brought the children along with them, and the other parent would then move heaven and earth to get them back, resulting in epic custody battles. The most implacable enemies the Shakers faced were parents who — like families today whose kids become Moonies or Hare Krishnas — feared that their children had been brainwashed and were determined to liberate them.

The Shakers often quoted Jesus. "I am come to set a man . . . against his father, and the daughter against her mother . . . and a man's foes shall be they of his own household."[12] Shakers' foes were often of their "own household." The Shaker village of Pleasant Hill in Kentucky was stormed by an armed mob, hundreds strong, led by the mother of a young woman named Lucy Bryant, whose father had brought her to the Shakers. Although Lucy Bryant protested that she was "stedfast and determind to stay" with the Shakers, she was forcibly hauled away.[13]

Others, like Lucy, were dragged from their new Shaker homes, literally kicking and screaming. Henry Blinn noted that, "Mary Howarth who was kidnapped last fall, from the Trustee's office, returns today having clandestinely left her parents." He added later, "She was again kidnapped in 1864."[14]

Sometimes the violence reached tragic levels. In 1863, Henry wrote that a Shaker named Caleb M. Dyer, "was shot by a returned soldier, (Thomas Wiers) . . . The affair was in relation to some children, living in the Church family. Wiers was tried and sentenced to 35 years in the State's Prison." Henry added sadly that "Caleb died on the 21st."[15]

～

But in spite of controversy and violence, the young Shaker villages were growing larger and larger. Too many people, though, could make logistics cumbersome and hard to manage — at one point the overcrowded Canterbury Shakers had to have three seatings for every meal. So when a village grew too large, it was divided into "families" — which had nothing to do with biological families. Each family numbered anywhere from a dozen to about a hundred and fifty people, settled into their own collection of Dwelling Houses and outbuildings, a mile or so away from the original settlement.

Canterbury in its heyday had four families, named for their location in reference to the Meeting House. The North Family was the "gathering order," for probationers, the "Young Believers" — who were not necessarily children. Shakers judged depth and commitment of belief to be more important than age, so that a "young" Believer might be a senior citizen. The beginners lived apart and were shepherded by experienced leaders. Those most committed to the "gospel life" eventually moved to the main village and joined the Church Family. It was a mark of Henry Blinn's mature convictions that as a teenager he was welcomed into this "senior" order.

Inadvertently, the Elders who came up with this system were following a principle known as "The Rule of 150." Sociologists argue that one hundred and fifty is approximately the number of people with whom any one person can maintain stable social relationships. From New Guinea to Greenland, hunter-gatherer societies tend to number fewer than 150; military organizations, from Roman legions to the US Marines, have always split vast armies into small, tight-knit groups. When there are fewer than 150 individuals, argues Malcolm Gladwell, a modern-day sociologist, the group can be controlled and organized on the basis of direct person-to-person relationships.[16]

Modern corporations like Gore Associated, makers of Goretex, take advantage of this concept. "People used to ask me, how do you do your long-term planning?" said a Gore executive. "And I'd say, that's easy, we put a hundred and fifty parking spaces in the lot, and when people start parking on the grass, we know it's time to build a new plant."[17]

Another Gore associate adds: "Peer pressure is much more powerful than a concept of a boss. Many, many times more powerful. People want to live up to what is expected of them."[18]

The Shakers intuitively grasped this idea. As Gladwell comments: "If you wanted to bring about a fundamental change in people's belief and behavior, a change that would persist and serve as an example to others, you needed to create a community around them, where those new beliefs could be practiced and expressed and nourished."[19] The Shakers, without benefit of modern sociological analysis, built a system with efficiency and effectiveness rivaling twenty-first-century corporations.

As any good boss knows, it's easier to get people to work hard if you pitch in there with them, sleeves rolled up, hands dirty. A silver-haired Elder could often be seen working beside his flock, getting in the hay or white-washing the Meeting House. When Henry Blinn was made an Elder, in addition to his considerable administrative responsibilities, he was expected to get busy in the tailor shop and learn to sew on buttons. This sharing of work led to a powerful spirit of community.

All Shakers were governed by the Central Ministry at New Lebanon, but each village had a good deal of autonomy, with its own set of Elders, who oversaw the community's spiritual life while Deacons organized the tasks of farm and workshop. And, as the pillars of the Church were Jesus and Mother Ann, so the pillars of each village were male and female, reflecting God's holy duality. Nearly all positions of Shaker leadership were shared by a man and a woman, so that there were Elders and Eldresses, Deacons and Deaconesses. Trustees, who had dealings with the World, were the one position that was male-dominated in the Shakers' early days.

The Shakers developed a true communal society. All property was owned in common, and each person participated in the work according to his ability, taking resources according to his need. Frederick Engels, the German philosopher who co-authored the *Communist Manifesto* with Karl Marx, noted the Shakers' unique brand of communism with interest.

The farmers, blacksmiths, bakers, and seamstresses who were flocking to the society possessed more than religious fervor and good intentions. They had the muscle and the practical skills needed for economic survival. The question now confronting the Elders was how to create a community wherein people of diverse personalities and backgrounds could live together in close proximity. And that meant that there had to be rules.

∼

There must be no unnecessary conversation after evening meeting, and none in bed . . .

Brethren and sisters are not allowed to read news-papers on saturday evening after supper, nor on the sabbath day . . .

Cucumbers are not to be eaten at any time, unless they are seasoned with pepper or salt, or both . . .

When brethren or sisters go up or down stairs they should not slip their feet on the carpet, but take them up and set them down plumb, so as not to wear out the carpets unnecessarily . . .

Fruit and vegetables must not be gathered on the sabbath except in case of necessity . . .

When we clasp our hands together our right thumbs & fingers should be above the left . . .[20]

❧

Being a Shaker, as Henry Blinn soon found, meant following the rules. In the early days of Shakerism, the regulations varied considerably from village to village and were open to interpretation by the different Elders and Eldresses. "Mother Lucy" Wright, who led the Shakers after Joseph Meacham died, was reluctant to have rules and regulations written down, lest they become too inflexible. But shortly after her death in 1821, the new ministry began sending out written copies of the "Orders and Rules of the Church at New Lebanon." These were considerably extended in 1845, and included more than a hundred acts that were "contrary to order." They were dubbed the "Millennial Laws."[21]

Any society needs laws, and many of these were sensible precautions dealing with health, hygiene, thrift, safety, and the humane treatment of animals. But there were certainly a lot of rules — and they must have been irksome. From the beginning, there were strict controls on what the Shakers innocently referred to as "Intercourse between the Sexes." It was contrary to order for a Brother to pass a Sister on the stairs; for Brothers and Sisters to talk together in the halls; for Brethren to shake hands or touch the Sisters, and vice versa; for the Brothers to go into the room when the Sisters made the beds. [22]

The young Henry Blinn had to deal with the reality of living under these precise laws. For him, as for many Shakers, it must have been a constant struggle to conform to such exact parameters for living. So . . . what would happen if the boy crossed his left thumb over his right, picked an apple on Sunday, or passed a Sister on the stairs? What would happen if, as he grew, he chose to wear a five-inch beard, or recklessly twirl his moustache? What punishment, penance, or mortification would be his?

❧

"Once I served God through fear," Ann Lee had said. "But now I serve him by love."[23] Rather than punishment, the Shakers believed in confession. Mother Ann apparently had a genius both for identifying troubled souls and for encouraging them to unburden themselves; after her death, Shaker leaders followed that tradition.

When the Believers at Hancock, Massachusetts, one of the first Shaker villages, were organizing, Joseph Meacham sent a deputation of Elders from New Lebanon to see if the new converts were spiritually prepared. After talking with them, Elder Henry Clough declared that someone in the group was concealing a secret sin.

The other Elders scolded Henry for discouraging promising converts. But "while they were speaking a brother came requesting the privilege of opening his mind . . . After the confession and repentance of this one, the gift of confession and cleansing from sin prevailed in such manner as had never before been known among them."[24] Sure enough, there wasn't a soul who didn't have a "secret sin" on their conscience.

Long before the science of psychology, Shakers understood the power of confession. In the repressed Puritan society of New England, they encouraged those with the guilt of hidden sins festering in their minds to let it all out, put the fear and torment into words, confide in one another. Mother Ann, with her gift for vivid metaphor, put it bluntly. "It is the heart which God looks at. The heart, with its hidden abominations, covered and concealed from the witnesses of Christ, becomes like a cage of unclean birds, and can never be cleansed short of a full and free confession."[25]

Even in modern times this remained a feature of Shaker life. Sister Frances Carr, a twenty-first-century Shaker, wrote of the "opening of the mind" as she had known it in her childhood.[26] This spiritual cleansing was not only good for the soul, but for the psychological and physical health of the Shakers as well.

This helps explain how a talented, creative, even rebellious person could live under such a strict regime. Those with overlong beards or incorrectly crossed thumbs were encouraged to make confession to an Elder. No one was forcibly shaved; no preachers announced the names of sinners in meeting. There was doubtless strong peer pressure to toe the line, but there were no stocks, irons, or dunce caps; no whips; no jails.

$\backsim$

Of course, a life of self-denial, rules, and hard work was not for everyone. Those who couldn't deal with it were asked to leave — or allowed to leave. There were no locks in Shaker villages to keep people incarcerated. Shaker record books routinely mention those who left, or "apostasized." Henry Blinn patiently recorded the years of Canterbury's many arrivals and departures, under the headings "Received" and "Removed."

Some couldn't stand the hard work that was every Shaker's lot. "William Shaw left the community of Shakers to shirk for himself," one Brother snapped.[27] Some just weren't a good fit, and rebellious souls caused frequent tension. A good deal of emotion is repressed in the terse notation in a Pleasant Hill journal: "Lucy Lemon was kindly invited to go to the World. She went!"[28]

Elder Grove Wright wrote scornfully of "*bad fish* caught in the Gospel net."[29] It was often a bitter disappointment when promising converts left. He had hard words for a whole family, the Whites, who had turned out to be back-sliders. "What can be more grievous and heart rending than to have those whoom [sic] we have placed confidence in as helps, prove traitors, and further do all in their power to destroy others. The Whites have proved themselves rotten hearted, and have all gone . . ."[30]

The authors of the *Testimonies* commented acidly that those who left the Shakers tended to be "distinguished by judgments, beyond what falls to the ordinary lot of mortals."[31] They recorded the dreadful fates that happened to some of the apostates, with a rather self-righteous attitude of "I-told-you-so." "Olive Warner went off, from Shirley, to the brothel in Boston, & rotted alive, as it were, with the venereal disease. James Burt went off and shot himself . . . Jeremiah Willard went off, and became a drunken sot, and is gone down to the grave . . ."[32]

But if Jeremiah Willard, William Shaw, Lucy Lemon, and others departed, many stayed. In the decades following Mother Ann's death, Shaker membership steadily increased. At the Shakers' peak, from four to six thousand Believers followed the "straight little narrow way." The Believers spread the gospel and established villages north in the pine forests of Maine, along the Eastern seaboard, west to the untamed lands of Ohio and Indiana, and as far south as the Kentucky hills. The "shining tree" that Brother James had foreseen was taking root in the New World, and flourishing.

Notes

[1] Cohen, Joel, editor. *Simple Gifts: Shaker Chants and Spirituals,* p. 24. This excerpt is from a traditional song known as "Virgins Cloth'd in a Clean White Garment."

[2] Blinn, *Record,* vol. 1, p. 295.

[3] Ibid., p. 298.

[4] *Testimonies,* p. 220.

[5] Burns, Deborah. *Shaker Cities of Peace, Love and Union.* Hanover, NH: University Press of New England, 1993, p. 33.

[6] The Millerites, led by William Miller, claimed that the date of Christ's Second Coming was revealed in Bible prophecy, and attracted more than 50,000 fervent believers. Miller first claimed that Christ would return between March of 1843 and March of 1844, but after the eagerly-awaited year had passed, Samuel S. Snow, a Millerite minister, set a final date of October 22, 1844.

[7] Cummins, Roger William. "The Second Eden: Charles Lane and American Transcendentalism," A Thesis Submitted to the Faculty of the Graduate School of the University of Minnesota, 1967, p. 278.

[8] Cheever, Susan. *American Bloomsbury: Louisa May Alcott, Ralph Waldo Emerson, Margaret Fuller, Nathaniel Hawthorne, and Henry David Thoreau: Their Lives, Their Loves, Their Work.* New York, NY: Simon and Schuster, Inc, 2006, p. 66.

[9] Alcott, Louisa May. *Transcendental Wild Oats.* Harvard, MA: The Harvard Common Press, 1975, p. 22. Louisa May Alcott's biting short story tells the history of Fruitlands in hilarious detail. After the collapse, Lane went to live at the nearby Shaker village for a while, though he never became a full-fledged Shaker.

[10] Ibid., p. 19.

[11] *Testimonies,* p. 222.

[12] *Holy Bible,* Matthew 10:35–6.

[13] Stein, *Shaker Experience,* p. 98.

[14] Blinn, *Record*, vol. 1, p. 184.

[15] Ibid., vol. 1, p. 187. Caleb Dyer was a Trustee of Enfield Shaker Village in New Hampshire. Thomas Weir, also recorded as Weirs, had placed his two young daughters with the Enfield Shakers at the time of his enlistment, agreeing to leave them there as long as they wished to stay. After being discharged from the army he sought to get his daughters back. After the Shakers repeatedly refused to return the children, Weir encountered Caleb Dyer in the road in front of the main office of the Shaker village, and deliberately shot him. Weir was convicted of murder.

[16] Gladwell, Malcolm. *The Tipping Point*. Boston, MA: Little, Brown and Co., 2000, p. 180.

[17] Ibid., p. 185.

[18] Ibid., p. 186.

[19] Ibid., p. 173.

[20] Kirk, John T. *The Shaker World: Art, Life, Belief*. New York, NY: Harry N. Abrams, Inc., 1997, pp. 261–264.

[21] Stein, *Shaker Experience*, p. 95.

[22] Kirk, John T., *The Shaker World*, p. 262.

[23] *Testimonies*, p. 345.

[24] White, Anna, and Leila S. Taylor. *Shakerism: Its Meaning and Message*. Columbus, OH: Press of Fred J. Heer, 1905, p. 83.

[25] *Testimonies*, p. 247.

[26] Carr, Frances. *Growing Up Shaker*. Sabbathday Lake, ME: United Society of Shakers, 1995, p. 98.

[27] Sprigg, *By Shaker Hands*, p. 24.

[28] Morse, *Shakers and the World's People*, p. 128.

[29] Brewer, Priscilla J. *Shaker Communities, Shaker Lives*. Hanover, NH: University Press of New England, 1986, p. 139.

[30] Burns, *Shaker Cities*, p. 141.

[31] *Testimonies*, p. 396.

[32] Ibid.

Laboring for the Lord

Who will bow, and bend like a willow,
Who will turn and twist and reel?
In the gale of simple freedom,
From the bower of Union flowing
Who will drink the wine of freedom
Dropping down like a shower
Pride and bondage all forgetting.

— Shaker song[1]

When the young Henry Blinn arrived at Canterbury, he must have been amazed at the magnitude of the plainly-dressed Shakers' place of residence. A "village" sounds like a quaint little cluster of cottages, but Henry's new home was built on a grander scale than its name implied. Canterbury was developing into a vast enterprise, covering thousands of acres, where hundreds of people lived and worked. The newly-expanded four-story Dwelling House, topped by a jaunty bell tower, was an elegantly designed mansion with more than fifty rooms. The massive Great Barn, built after Henry's arrival, was the largest in New Hampshire, a monumental construction of stone and wood, 250 feet long. The village was packed with many other buildings as well: barns, dairy, laundry, workshops, and outbuildings, painted in bright, eye-catching hues, and humming like beehives with state-of-the-art equipment.

It must have been easy to overlook a small, white-washed building that stood apart, on the edge of the bustling village. But this modest structure was the hub of the village, the very core of Shaker life.

The Meeting House was a neat, white rectangle, perfect in its symmetry, topped off by twin brick chimneys. There was a Brothers' door at one end, a Sisters' door at the other, so that men and women could enter on equal terms — but forever separated. Almost every Shaker village had a similar building, and when Henry traveled as an older man, he could recognize them at a glance; the Millennial Laws stated that "No buildings may be painted white, save meeting houses."[2] When he went from village to village, as Elders often did, he would most likely worship in a place as homelike and familiar as the one he had grown up in.

The elegant little buildings were the work of Moses Johnson, an eighteenth-century New Hampshire builder who designed and oversaw construction of Meeting Houses for nearly a dozen Shaker villages. The Meeting Houses are practically identical, down to the last pegboard; all are built in classic New England style. (A few villages, however, had Meeting Houses constructed in a different style, notably the massive Meeting House at New Lebanon, a barrel-roofed ballroom which could hold more than a thousand people.)

A Meeting House was described by a contemporary visitor as being "of beautiful workmanship, painted inside a glossy Prussian blue . . . from the neatness of every thing one would suppose the whole house was washed between every meeting day."[3] Often the Meeting House was the first new building constructed at a site — Canterbury's formal "call to order" in the summer of 1792 was marked by the construction of the community's place of worship. But these modest, white buildings were frequently the serene eye at the center of a hurricane.

In August, 1831, the *Salem Gazette* described the scene outside a Shaker Meeting House on Sunday morning: "a large number of carriages of various kinds were ranged along the fence, most of them from the neighboring towns, but some from a considerable distance, and all freighted with curious visitors."[4] People came from far and wide to see the show put on by the singing, dancing Shakers; it was not unheard of for a public service to have five hundred spectators.

The Shakers had decidedly mixed feelings about this inquisitive audience, who must have sometimes jammed the Meeting House doorways and gaped through the windows. Since Mother Ann's day, visitors had been welcomed in the hope that they would convert. But so many tourists came "more to gratify an idle curiosity, and spend the day for their own amusement, than to respect the solemn worship of a pure & holy God," that the Shakers finally resorted to putting a notice in the newspapers, announcing that worship would be closed for a time, except to those who "honestly and sincerely seek for information."[5]

But usually, the Shakers felt it was their duty to spread the gospel and encourage converts, so they gritted their teeth and put up with it. Indeed, they put benches around the inside of the Meeting Houses for the express purpose of comfortably accommodating visitors — though men were required to sit separately from women. Contemporary illustrations show the benches tightly packed with richly-dressed spectators. The famous and the humble, the idle and the curious: thousands of the World's people came to laugh, to wonder, and to criticize. The Marquis de Lafayette paid a visit in 1784, and, intrigued, stayed to talk with Shakers after the service. James Fenimore Cooper and Nathaniel Hawthorne visited, as did Ralph Waldo Emerson and Herman Melville, who mentioned the Shakers, unflatteringly, in *Moby Dick*. Charles Dickens was hugely miffed at having been turned away during one of the rare periods when spectators were not allowed. To this day, the World's people are welcomed to the Shakers' Sunday morning services.

༄

Henry's Sabbath would have started out conventionally enough. The Believers rose early on Sunday morning, put on their best, and when the bell rang, went to worship, just as he had done in the World. But the Shakers wore special garments to their services. Henry might have donned a blue vest — blue being the color of the celestial heavens — and soft, light dancing slippers.

He would have lined up with the other males, and entered by the Brother's entrance, while the Sisters filed in through the other door. Henry, when he first arrived as a boy, doubtless tagged along at the end of the line. After a period of silent prayer, some singers would start a tune, and the others would dance. The service might go on for an hour or much more, and if you've ever participated in a brisk session of aerobics, you'll know why the dance was often referred to as "laboring." The serenity of the dancers must have been sorely tried by the irreverence of the watchers. Elders sometimes had to speak up and admonish the audience to stop laughing.

"I'll take nimble steps, I'll be a David!" the Shakers sang, recalling how the biblical David had danced for joy before the Ark of the Covenant.[6] The original untrammeled worship had been highly individual, each person moving as the spirit directed: rolling on the ground, leaping in the air, spinning wildly, or merely sitting in a chair and singing. But by the time Henry Blinn joined the Shakers, the services had become a more formalized ritual.

Joseph Meacham first introduced a choreographed dance, which he called the "Holy Order;" it was also known, more enticingly, as the "Square Order Shuffle." Worship services almost became performances, with well-rehearsed movements done in unison. Later, as "Mother Ann's Work" got underway, the worship became less structured, as the dance was interrupted by visits and revelations from the spirit world, and during this period the services were sometimes closed to the public.

But nothing ever blotted out the passion, or the enthusiasm, of Shaker worship. Photographs of Henry Blinn show a prim, proper gentleman, in formal attire; it's hard to imagine him singing and dancing. But the Shakers danced with energy (Figure 4). Elder Joseph Brackett, author of the famous song *Simple Gifts*, was remembered as spinning about "with his coat tails a-flying."[7]

There were few worse sins to the original settlers of New England than dancing. Puritans had inveighed against the evils of

Figure 4. "Wilder and louder swells the music," Horace Greeley, the famous journalist, wrote in 1838, the year Henry Blinn joined the dance. "Quicker and more intricate becomes the 'labor.' Now all are prancing around the room . . . to a melody as lively as Yankee Doodle." Use courtesy of Shaker Museum and Library, Old Chatham and New Lebanon, NY.

"the daunce" since Elizabethan times.[8] The Pilgrim Fathers and Mothers of Plymouth did not dance, but viewed with suspicion their "savage" Native American neighbors, who definitely did.[9] One of the distinguishing marks of witches was that they danced in Satan's worship. In seventeenth-century Salem, people were hanged for that crime.

Even by the time Henry joined the Shakers, in the more enlightened nineteenth century, many people still considered dancing to be a scandalous pastime — especially for women. Young folks with permissive parents might indulge in dancing on a Saturday night, but it was surely not for Sunday morning.

But the Shakers, from their early days, danced. The names of Shaker dances give an idea of what the scene looked like: Lively Line, Double Square, Cross and Diamond, Moving Square, Elder Benjamin's Cross. It must have been a bit like a good, old-fashioned square-dance — and it sounds like fun. "In meeting four hours," wrote a Massachusetts Shaker. "We have a blessed good time."[10]

The Shakers sang, too. Pictures or descriptions of Shaker rituals may seem dry and uninspiring because they lack the beauty of the soaring melodies that energized them. Instruments were banned until well after the Civil War — the human voice was the only music. The Meeting Houses were designed for excellent acoustics, and the holy songs rang out magnificently.

Listen to a good recording of Shaker music — in authentic style, not a sentimentalized version with violin accompaniment — and you'll soon find your toe tapping. You might even find yourself humming along.[11] These melodies are meant for singing, not only during worship but also at work in the fields, at the loom, or while kneading bread in the kitchen.

Some Shaker music may seem sweetly familiar to you, and if so it's because much of it was adapted from English or early American melodies with strong, danceable rhythms. These traditional folk tunes were familiar to the Shakers as they still are to many of us today, melodies like "Barbara Allan" and "Yankee Doodle;" "Shady Grove," an Appalachian fiddle tune; or "The Three Ravens," an ancient English ballad. Surprisingly light-hearted songs, such as "Oh, Dear, What Can the Matter Be?" and "The Girl I Left Behind Me" metamorphosed into heart-felt hymns.[12]

To these melodies the Shakers added symbolic movements, and if young Henry forgot the steps, the words of the song could remind him of what came next. "When true simplicity is gaind [sic], to bow and to bend we shan't be asham'd. To turn, turn, will be our delight, 'till by turning, turning we come round right." The well-known words of "Simple Gifts" were, in part, choreography.

The singing was punctuated by clapping and stamping. "Wilder and louder swells the music," Horace Greeley, the famous journalist, wrote in 1838, the year Henry Blinn joined the dance. "Quicker and more intricate becomes the 'labor.' Now all are prancing around the room, in double file, to a melody as lively as Yankee Doodle."[13] Shakers enacted stamping out Satan, and shaking away lust and temptation. And it must have been easier to sleep sweetly, without yearning for the "gratification of the flesh" after a sweaty, energetic workout. Greeley, a perceptive observer, described a service as "the battle-ground of a war against all carnal impulses."[14]

Most of the spectators went away, giggling, scornful, or disgusted. But some people, like Henry and thousands of others before and after his time, found that the dance and the music lingered in the mind. They were aware that there was deeply-felt emotion behind the odd ritual.

Sister Lillian Phelps came to Canterbury as a young girl in 1892, and passed away in 1973, after more than 80 years as a Shaker. She was one of the last souls to have participated in the traditional Shaker dance. Sister Lillian recalled wistfully: "There was a definite psychological purpose behind the Shaker marches, seldom explained, and rarely understood by the general Public. The perfect rhythmic body motions of a worshipper, who combined this activity with a deep mental and religious fervor, developed within himself a great spiritual inspiration, almost impossible to understand or describe, by one who has never witnessed or participated in this form of worship. But if one could have been present as I was, and could have seen the perfect spiritual union, that was produced, when a soul combined the physical motions, the singing voice and the dedicated heart."[15]

Physical motion, the singing voice, and the dedicated heart . . . this "great spiritual inspiration" was the bedrock of Shaker life. As Lillian Phelps, the kidnapped Lucy Bryant, Henry Blinn, and many others found, the spiritual outlet of the Meeting House — the ecstasy of encountering God in that little white-washed building — was what kept many Shakers steadfast and determined to stay.

This phenomenon may be difficult for a twenty-first-century person to understand. But perhaps anyone who has ever danced on a chair at a rock concert, or cruised down the highway with the volume cranked up on the radio, exceeding the speed limit in a kind of sweet madness, has had a glimpse of what the Shakers were all about.

Notes

[1] Cohen, Joel, editor. *Simple Gifts: Shaker Chants and Spirituals*, p. 46. A song known as "Laughing John's Interrogatory," ca. 1840. "Laughing John was an African-American spirit, familiar to the Shakers of New Hampshire and Maine."

[2] Andrews, Edward Deming. *The People Called Shakers*. New York, NY: Dover Publications, Inc., 1963, p. 285.

[3] W. S. Warder, *A Brief Sketch of the Religious Society of People Called Shakers*, London, 1818, quoted in Burns, *Shaker Cities*, p. 32.

[4] *Salem Gazette*, 1831, August 5, quoted in Horgan, Edward R. *The Shaker Holy Land: A Community Portrait*. Boston, MA: The Harvard Common Press, 1987, p. 72.

[5] Blinn, *Record*, vol. 1, p. 33.

[6] Patterson, *Shaker Spiritual*, p. 254.

[7] Eldress Caroline Helfrich, quoted in Patterson, *Shaker Spiritual*, p. 373.

[8] Pennino-Baskerville, Mary. "Terpsichore Reviled: Antidance Tracts in Elizabethan England." *Sixteenth Century Journal 1991*, vol. 22, no. 3, p. 475.

[9] Bradford, William. *Of Plymouth Plantation*. New York, NY: Random House, 1981, p.75.

[10] Sears, *Gleanings*, p. 227.

[11] See Christian Goodwillie, ed., *Shaker Songs: A Celebration of Peace, Harmony, and Simplicity*, New York, NY: Black Dog & Leventhal Publishers, Inc., 2002, and Cohen, Joel, ed., *Simple Gifts: Shaker Chants and Spirituals*, a Recording of Shaker Music by the Shakers of Sabbathday Lake and the Boston Camerata. 1 Audio CD, Erato Disques, 1995. Both of these are beautiful and historically accurate renderings of Shaker music. See also *http://www.bostoncamerata.org.*

[12] In a similar fashion, many ancient tunes have metamorphosed into beloved Christmas carols like "Deck the Halls with Boughs of Holly," or "Good King Wenceslas" — the holiday words were added centuries after the rollicking secular tunes were written.

[13] Horace Greeley, "A Sabbath with the Shakers," *New York Monthly Magazine*, June 1838, quoted in Morse, *Shakers and the World's People*, p. 159.

[14] Ibid.

[15] Phelps, Lillian. *Shaker Music; A Brief History*. Canterbury, NH: Published by the Canterbury Shakers, p. 5.

Love Made Visible

The winter's past, and the spring appears;
The turtle dove is in our land.
In yonder's valley there grows sweet union.
Let us arise, and take our fill.

— Shaker song[1]

The Dwelling House at Hancock Shaker Village stands spacious and solid, built of warm red brick with innumerable windows. The dining hall, meeting room, and several of the retiring rooms are open for viewing by the public; they are elegant rooms, with pale walls and beautiful wooden trim and flooring — modest, serene places for the Brethren and Sisters to pass their days in meditation and prayer.

On a recent visit, I walked into one of the small bedrooms — and then staggered back, half blinded with the brilliance of the light. This room wasn't like all the others; this room had walls as white as snow, trimmed with a vivid lemon yellow that Van Gogh might have envied. The wooden planks of the floor were painted a deep, glowing red. "They've ruined it!" was my first thought. "What kind of vandals would splash paint on all that beautiful oak and maple?"

But the costumed interpreter who worked at the museum assured me that this was, according to the most up-to-date microscopic analysis and painstaking research, the way nineteenth-century Shakers painted their rooms.

"It's awfully bright, isn't it?" I said blinking in the flood of sunshine that poured through the crystal-clear windows and bounced off all those primary colors. "Looks a bit like Toys R Us."

"Well," she said, considering. "They were a happy people."

⤬

"If I owned the whole world, I would turn it all into joyfulness," said Ann Lee. With her unique blend of ecstasy and hardheaded practicality, she added, "I would not say to the poor, *Be ye warmed, and be ye clothed,* without giving them wherewith to do it."[2]

For every person, male or female, young or old, the Shaker life was a life of hard work. The wherewithal for warming, clothing, and feeding a village of several hundred people involved long days of backbreaking labor, hours of careful planning, and strict discipline. But the Shaker religion did not put rigid barriers between the times of worship and the times of work; joyfulness was not reserved for the Meeting House on Sunday mornings.

Henry Blinn wrote that "the worship of God is not wholly confined to one particular building, but the soul of the devout Believer is mindful of his duty at all times and in all places."[3] He would have agreed with the Lebanese poet Kahlil Gibran, a world and a century away, that "work is love made visible."[4]

The huge Dwelling House at Canterbury (Figure 5) was where Henry Blinn and his Brothers and Sisters began their day. It might have been hard for him, occasionally, to be "mindful of duty" when the Rising Bell clanged at half-past four in the morning. There were lazy Shakers, of course: "Old Slugs" who would lie abed in the morning rather than warm their souls with labor. But most Shakers came from a background of middle-class farms and villages, where early rising and hard work were the norm. The Believers would climb out of their warm beds, and get dressed near a small stove, then head out in the gray morning light to begin the day's work. A Brother might pitch hay, milk the cows, carry water, and muck out the stalls — all before breakfast.

Figure 5. When the young Henry Blinn arrived at Canterbury, he must have been amazed at the magnitude of the plainly-dressed Shakers' place of residence. The newly-expanded, four-story Dwelling House, topped by a jaunty bell tower, was an elegantly designed mansion with more than fifty rooms. Use courtesy of Shaker Museum and Library, Old Chatham and New Lebanon, NY.

While the Brethren tended to the outdoor chores, the Sisters got to work in the kitchen. The Shakers are often, rightly, hailed for their progressive attitudes involving women, but still, this was not exactly "women's liberation" as we know it today. Shakers, like Native Americans, recognized certain types of work as exclusively women's work; other tasks were declared men's work. Women cooked. Men plowed. Women cleaned the bedrooms, men cleaned the barns. Sisters were not shielded from hard labor, by any means — kneading dough for five dozen loaves of bread certainly required plenty of muscle-power, but no Brother would pitch in.

Often male and female work combined to create a satisfying whole: women wove baskets, men made the wooden handles; men crafted chairs, women wove the colorful wool tapes used for seats. Brothers sheared the sheep, Sisters spun the wool. And the men (literally) brought home the bacon at hog-butchering time, and the women cooked it.

The earliest Shakers had known hard times and empty bellies. Sister Rebecca Clarke recalled some dismal menus from her first days as a Believer, in the late 1700s. "We lived mostly upon bean porridge and water porridge. Monday morning we had a little weak tea, and once a week a small piece of cheese . . . When I look back to those days, and then to the fullness with which we are blessed, it fills me with thankfulness."[5]

By the time Henry Blinn joined the Shakers, the Sisters who descended to the cool basement kitchen in the morning had many causes to be thankful. Every season brought its bounty; perusing a book of traditional Shaker recipes is enough to make your mouth water. Breakfast in summer might include cherry muffins, huckleberry griddle cakes, or, in June, strawberry shortcake; in fall, it would be time for apple pancakes, apple dumplings and that classic New England staple, apple pie. Winter brought fresh-made sausages, and in March, the sweet taste of maple syrup; in spring, when the calves were born, came the richest cream for buttermilk cornbread or creamed oysters.

The Sisters shared kitchen duties in monthly rotations. In the big Dwelling Houses like the one at Canterbury, they worked in squads of ten or so at a time, with young girls learning from the older women. Their kitchen was state-of-the-art. Shakers were famous for their wizardry at creating labor-saving devices: mechanical apple-parers, apple-corers, double rolling pins designed to roll the dough twice as thin and twice as fast. A Canterbury Sister, Emmeline Hart, designed an enormous oven with four-foot-long rotating racks that could bake sixty loaves of bread at once.

In Shaker kitchens, ranges and ovens were often enclosed or shielded so that the Sisters' long gowns could not be set aflame. "Skirt fires" were a leading cause of horrible injuries and death in the days of hearth cooking. The emphasis on kitchen safety was yet another measure of the value Shakers placed on women.

The Sisters rang the breakfast bell promptly at six. Elder Frederick Evans, a New Lebanon Shaker, described mealtime. "A big dining-room, which they enter in two files, one composed of the brethren, from the oldest in regular gradation of age down to the youngest, and led by the elders, the other composed of the sisters, from the oldest down to the youngest, and led by the eldresses . . . Arrived at their places, they all kneel for a moment in silent thanksgiving and prayer. Then all seat themselves and eat the meal with speechless assiduity."[6]

After a hearty breakfast, the Shakers headed off to field, kitchen, or workshop well fueled for a morning's labor. But here again, the work was eased by their amazing inventiveness. Unlike the Amish, with whom they are frequently confused, the Shakers embraced technology. The Shaker villages that today are living history museums may look quaint and old-fashioned to modern eyes, but that's because they're generally "set," like a play, in the early nineteenth century. But Canterbury wasn't a sleepy farm, by any means. The village was humming and clanking with mechanical activity. "Considerable expense has been laid out on the waterworks," Henry noted in 1860. "A new flue boiler has been set up in the laundry and a tall chimney built for better draft. An extractor for drying clothes has been added to the machinery at the laundry, and this for the Sisters is a valuable addition."[7]

Real-life Shaker farms and workshops were anything but old-fashioned; they generally sported the very latest gadgets. Even in the 1700s, many buildings had running water, carried in underground pipes from distant ponds. A water-powered turbine was installed at Hancock in 1858, and it powered a vast array of saws, drills, and laundry machines. Canterbury Shakers had the first electricity in their area, years ahead of the local towns. They pioneered the first flush toilets in the region, and the first automobile. Visitors in the 1970s, when the last Shaker Sisters lived there, were often bemused to see television antennas poking out of classic Shaker buildings.

Shakers incessantly tinkered and fiddled, seeking ways of saving time and easing labor. It was a Shaker Brother who reinvented the most basic of household utensils: the broom.

Brooms had been, since the dawn of time — or at least the dawn of house-keeping — a round bunch of twigs or straw tied around a stick. In 1798, Brother Theodore Bates realized that flattening the straw into a tightly-bound, oblong bundle would enormously increase brooms' efficiency. The "Shaker broom" is the standard model used to this day.

Perhaps only in the freedom of a society like the Shakers' could both sexes have enjoyed such opportunities for creativity. It was a Sister, Tabitha Babbitt, who watched a carpenter using a hand saw and realized half his labor was wasted, since the upstroke cut no wood. Observing the smooth and efficient motion of her spinning wheel, she had an idea. She is credited by oral tradition with the invention of the first circular saw in the United States.[8]

Shaker ingenuity extended to every corner of life. Shaker horticulturists developed new and better varieties of plants. Shaker laundresses used new and improved irons, dryers, and clothespins. Shakers developed a vacuum evaporator for making herbal medicines, an idea that a Mr. Borden borrowed to make condensed milk — which he later marketed as light-weight, nutritious rations for Civil War soldiers, making him a fortune. Henry Blinn, an expert apiarist among his many other skills, made innovations to the ancient art of bee-keeping, coming up with a creative system of vents to "air-condition" his bee-hives and increase honey production in hot weather (Figure 6).

Many advances were made in the women's area of household chores. It was a Shaker Brother who invented the first industrial-sized washing machine, capable of washing many bedsheets at once. And if you think that this doesn't sound like an exciting victory for women's liberation, then you've never scrubbed sheets on a washboard, with your knuckles bleeding and your hands blistering in scalding water. Wool carders, knitting machines, mechanical bread kneaders, efficient butter churns, pea shellers, soup kettles: the Shakers were among the first to acknowledge that the drudgery of housework could and should be lightened, and that women's time was worth saving.

Shaker inventions were seldom patented, since the Shaker's creed was to share God's blessings, not profit from them, so patents

Figure 6. Even an Elder like Henry Blinn participated in the work of putting food on the table. Elder Henry was an expert and innovative bee-keeper. Use courtesy of Shaker Museum and Library, Old Chatham and New Lebanon, NY.

were considered selfish and prideful. However, the washing machine was one of the few inventions that was patented, and it was sold, very profitably, to large hotels.

Some of their inventions improved the lot of animals, too. Well-designed plows, rakes, and harrows eased the labor of draft horses and oxen. Shakers even pioneered the use of "have-a-heart" traps, in which mice could be caught alive and released unharmed.

The Shakers applied their orderly methods and ingenuity to cooking, as well. They wrote down recipes with precise measurements, in the era when cooking was generally an unscientific "pinch of this" and "a bit of that." Midday dinner was the big meal of the day, and the Sisters put a lot of work into it.

One of the factors that kept the young Henry Blinn a happy Shaker was the cuisine. He and other boys often spent the morning in the cropfields, supervised by a kindly Brother, and they worked up an appetite by dinnertime. "Hungry and tired as we sometimes were, and yet never too tired to run a full mile if we chanced to be that distance from home." Like all hungry youngsters, they watched the clock — except there was no clock to watch. "We would keep urging the good old man to tell us the hour of the day," Henry remembered, but as "no one except a Trustee would be expected to carry a watch . . . the sun was our only guide." The patient Brother would "time after time, stop his work in response to our importunings and, standing erect, pace on his shadow and tell us how long it would be before the bell would ring for the call to dinner.[9]

The Sisters rang the eagerly-awaited bell at the stroke of noon. Brothers, Sisters, boys, and girls would stream in from the fields and workshops; all would wash up, and then sit for a few minutes in quiet meditation. Then they entered the Dining Hall, to kneel behind their chairs in silent prayer.

The Shakers welcomed many guests, but required a high standard from visitors, who were expected to conform to Shaker ways. Publications called "table monitors" were made available to give guests, as well as Shakers, some guidelines. "All should sit upright at the table," one began. "When you cut meat, cut it square & equal, fat & lean, & take an equal proportion of bones...Eat what you need before you rise from table, and not be picking & eating afterwards." And, "if you are obliged to sneeze or cough," the monitor added testily, "don't bespatter the victuals, make use of your handkerchief."[10]

The Shakers' rule of eating meals in silence must have encouraged concentration on the food. And it was food well worth concentrating on: chicken pie, veal cutlets in sour cream, pork chops with mustard. Cold days were warmed by winter soup with onions and potatoes, or ham fritters with hot tartar sauce. Cooks were instructed to remember Mother Ann's directive to see that "your victuals is prepared in good order; that when the brethren come in from their hard work, they can bless you, and eat their food with thankfulness, without murmuring."[11]

It should be clear by now that the Shakers were far from ascetics when it came to meals. Desserts were often included in the menu: cider cake, maple sugar cake, frivolous delicacies like candied mint leaves, or the more solid brown sugar cherry cookies, blueberry cake, or honey pound cake with raisins. Ann Lee's birthday was traditionally celebrated with Mother Ann's Cake, rich with butter, eggs, and sugar.[12]

The Shakers were famous for their thrift. "Shaker your plate!" meant to eat every scrap. "When you have done eating, clean your plate, knife & fork," the table monitor instructed. "Lay your bones in a snug heap by the side of your plate — scrape up your crumbs."[13] The monitor's harshness was softened by the signs the Shakers sometimes posted, that read "We Make You Kindly Welcome."

Shaker meals were so good that many a wandering laborer suddenly became smitten with a desire to "embrace the gospel," join the Shakers, and enjoy three squares a day. Conversions were especially common in late autumn, when the farm work was least arduous. Celibacy was a high price to pay, however, even for a comfortable bed and well-cooked meals, and lukewarm converts often left in spring, when the work got heavy. This phenomenon was so common that such folk were called "winter Shakers" or "bread-and-butter Shakers." Those who joined not to hear the word of God but only to eat the loaves and fishes He provided, were scornfully known as "loafers." However, the Shakers did not turn them away, always hoping for another convert.

◆

In spite of the good food, it was a hard life, and the Shakers generally put in a long, tough day. But their lot was not so different from that of the average farmer of the era — and, ironically, in some ways the rigidly controlled Shaker life offered more freedom than that of the World. An ordinary laborer was tied to the same seasonal round of chores, year in, year out, but a Shaker Brother could try new careers, learn new skills from experts, and see if he had an aptitude for blacksmithing, stone-cutting, barbering, or clock-making.

Options for Sisters were more conventional. But there were possibilities for an ambitious woman beyond cooking, cleaning, and mending. She could try her hand at fine tailoring, weaving, basket-making, writing or teaching, or learn the healing arts and the use of medicinal herbs. And, with the Shakers, a woman could aspire to a position of real leadership, a chance for responsibility and author-ity that was all but impossible to attain in the World.

Young Shakers were assigned to a wide variety of tasks. Af-ter Henry's stint at pail-making, he was set to work in the black-smith shop, but when it was discovered the fourteen-year-old lacked the muscles for the arduous job, he was sent to the carding mill, where he learned to run the machines that prepared wool for weav-ing. Using brains rather than brawn, he soon rose from mill-hand to supervisor.

When the carding was done, he learned to "make and mend tinware." In between farm chores, he worked as a night-watchman and "headed broom-nails" before finally finding his preferred niche as a teacher.[14] He avoided teacher burn-out with bee-keeping and carpentry. He hated tailoring, but enjoyed the challenge of pulling teeth and designing false ones in his dentist's shop. He became expert at the trade of printing, and spent much time in writing.

Shakers were enthusiastic journal-keepers, and their diaries tell of the passing seasons. Brother Grove Wright's diary combines an artist's appreciation of color with a shrewd stocksman's eye for good forage. "The season uncommonly forward, apple trees look considerable green, and begin to show the red buds for blossoming; grass is up a pretty good bite."[15] Shaker journals tell of cracking butternuts or plucking turkeys in January, blackberrying in August. In winter it was time to fill the ice house and cut firewood; in March it was time to "fix for sugaring." April was planting — onions, wheat, oats, barley, carrots, corn, potatoes — and time to shear the sheep.

And when there was a big chore to do — raising a building, or getting in the hay — it was all hands to work.

✑

Most of the huge Shaker barns, like the one Henry Blinn knew at Canterbury, have collapsed or burned in one of the tragic fires that have claimed so many historic buildings. But the magnificent barn at the Hancock Shaker Village still stands, lovingly restored, to give us a sense of what Shaker work-days were like.

When visitors see the Round Stone Barn for the first time, they often conclude that the majestic building must be the Shaker church. They're not entirely wrong. When you enter the wide doors and look up, the ceiling is high overhead, with beams spreading out from the center in a circular pattern like the spokes of a wheel. Broad windows let in streams of light, and doves flutter in the rafters. The vast, airy space has the spiritual quality of a cathedral.[16]

As so often with the Shakers, spirituality and practicality were blended here. The barn was the ultimate in efficiency, brilliantly designed; it quickly became a showplace and tourist attraction, as it remains to this day. But in such a beautiful place, it must have been easy for the workers to feel that they were laboring in the fields of the Lord. An anonymous Shaker felt this keenly when he wrote that "Heaven and Earth are threads of one loom."[17]

The cylindrical building was designed around an enormous haymow, a tube of scaffolding about thirty-five-feet high and fifty-five-feet in diameter. Here was piled a huge mound of hay that filled the center of the barn two stories high, like the core of a great apple. Stanchions for cattle surrounded the tall haystack, so that more than fifty cows could stand in a circle, facing inwards. A Brother, walking a narrow path between cows and haystack, could pull hay from the pile and fork it over to the animals with a few efficient motions. Later, a manure pit was added, and manure was pitched down through a chute to the lower floor, eventually to be carried away and used for fertilizer.

The barn was built into the side of a hill, so that full advantage could be taken of gravity. At haying time, ox-drawn wagons, each bearing a shaggy grass mountain ten feet high, drove through an entrance on the second floor. The oxen plodded around a circular trackway, and paused while the Brethren forked the sweet-smelling hay *down* into the central haymow. Anyone who has ever spent a sweltering July afternoon heaving hay bales *up* into a loft, as is usually done, will hail this labor-saving ingenuity. Then the wagons continued around the circular floor and exited the barn without the difficult and dangerous task of backing up the oxen.

The fact that the Shakers could whistle up a hundred workers at a time gave them a tremendous economic edge over the neighboring family farms. Ten of the ponderous wagons could be unloaded simultaneously. At haying time the barn must have been like a giant bee-hive, with Brothers swarming over the huge piles of grass, the year's fragrant harvest piling up in the hay-mow, and holy song echoing from the high rafters.

∾

After a long afternoon's labor, it was time to rest; a calm half-hour set aside for meditation, then a light supper. Evening chores remained — for the Sisters, washing hundreds of cups and plates; for the Brothers, bedding down the livestock or carrying firewood. Then work was done for the day.

"All work and no play makes Jack a dull boy" runs the famous maxim that nineteenth-century children copied in their schoolbooks. The Shakers allowed time for weary laborers to unwind. The Elders early realized that fraternal affections could sometimes be more powerful than the lusts of the flesh, and so Union Meetings were held — and attendance was generally required — so that Brothers and Sisters could spend time together.

After supper, once or twice a week, small groups of Sisters would carry chairs across the hall, to be joined by the same number of Brothers. The chairs would be lined up facing each other, five feet apart — men on one side, women on the other. Then newcomers to the Shaker family would forge the bonds of friendship with informal chat, and old friends who had been Shakers for years would share memories and stories, laughter and jokes. Often they would sing together. Sometimes smoking was allowed, or refreshments like apples, nuts, and cider were enjoyed.[18] Sharp-eyed Elders, however, watched for any sign that romance was flowering, so they could nip it in the bud by promptly shifting those who were attracted to each other to different Union groups.

After the evening's festivities, it was off to bed. Shakers are often compared to monks and nuns, but unlike Catholic religious communities, Shakers of both genders shared the same dwelling. Entering one of the big Shaker Dwelling Houses is a little like going through the looking glass. There's an eerie sense of reflection, the way trees are reflected in the still surface of a pond. There are two doors, two stairways, two of everything. Each half of the building precisely mirrors the other; every door, cupboard, knob and peg on the men's side has a counterpart on the women's side. There are invariably two sets of pegboards on the walls — one to hold the Brothers' straw hats, another the Sisters' bonnets.

Behind the numbered, identical doors were the "retiring rooms." Henry Blinn, as a young Brother, would have shared a room with two or three other Brothers; Elders sometimes had private rooms. The chambers were simply furnished: a bed for each person, a chair or two, a stove, perhaps a writing desk. The ubiquitous pegboards created a precise line at shoulder height around the walls, with perhaps a broom or candle-holder hanging from a peg.

There were no velvet draperies to shroud the wide windows, no Oriental carpets to hide the shining floors; no pictures, knick-knacks, or dust-catchers. In the days of ornate Victorian excess, the World's stuffy, unventilated rooms often boasted loudly-patterned wallpaper, stained glass windows, and heavy drapes; household objects were fringed, flowered, and tasseled. The Shakers were often sneered at for being too poor or too stingy to spend money on furnishings.

Charles Dickens visited a Shaker village in 1842, and despised everything he saw. "We walked into a grim room, where several grim hats were hanging on grim pegs, and the time was grimly told by a grim clock, which uttered every tick with a kind of struggle, as if it broke the grim silence reluctantly, and under protest. Ranged against the wall were six or eight stiff high-backed chairs, and they partook so strongly of the general grimness, that one would much rather have sat on the floor than incurred the smallest obligation to any of them."[19]

Today, few people would agree with his assessment. But more than a century had to pass before the rest of the world caught up with the Shakers and began to appreciate the healthfulness of their sunny, well-ventilated spaces, or the austere beauty of their buildings' clean, uncluttered lines.

❧

At the end of a long day, Henry Blinn would climb into his narrow, and lonely, bed. A formal man, he rarely confided his innermost thoughts and emotions to his journal. We can never know if he occasionally wondered what it would be like to share a bed with the soft, warm body of a woman.

Celibacy was a challenge, no doubt about it. The Shakers realized it was a sacrifice that not everyone was prepared to make, and while they certainly condemned lust and extra-marital fornication, they did not regard marriage as a sinful state. They referred to celibacy as "bearing the full cross," the mark of a true Believer. It was their one rule that was ironclad and unchanging. "It is the earthly, fleshly, *relation* that must be hated by all," Elder Frederick Evans wrote. "Jesus said, 'They neither marry nor are given in marriage, but are as angels of God in heaven.'"[20]

Temptation, however, was always near at hand — right across the hall. Only an invisible line down the middle of the buildings divided Brothers and Sisters. "We do carry out sexual purity, notwithstanding that the sexes are brought face to face, in everyday life," Evans proudly pointed out, "yet living without bolts or bars, in the same household of faith."[21]

Inevitably, a certain amount of backsliding went on. Shakers, of course, were not "angels of God in heaven," but merely human beings, and there were no locks on retiring-room doors. Not infrequently, couples sneaked out of the Dwelling House late at night; sometimes they never came back, but returned to the World to marry.

The "cross" seems always to have been easier for women to bear. By Henry Blinn's time, Sisters already outnumbered Brothers; in a few decades would come the day when there were ten female Shakers for every male — and finally, no male Shakers at all. In an era when birth control was virtually nonexistent, and childbirth had a high mortality rate, there must have been many women who did not find chastity a hardship.

But, hardship or not, celibacy was a way of life chosen by many thousands of Shakers, both male and female. Those like Henry, who came as children, were dedicated to virginity for their entire lives.

❧

When Henry Blinn climbed into his solitary bed and blew out the candle, the Dwelling House around him grew silent, except for an occasional snore from a hundred tired sleepers. An even greater hush surrounded the village on the moonlit hill. For miles around, there stretched silent green forests, and meadows where only the night wind rustled the grass. The village was remote from the World, wrapped in tranquility. The peace must have seemed as though it would last forever.

Notes

[1] Patterson, *Shaker Spiritual*, p. 69. One of the earliest Shaker songs, known as "Father James's song."

[2] *Testimonies*, p. 270.

[3] Ott, John Harlow. *Hancock Shaker Village: A Guidebook and History.* Hancock, MA: Shaker Community, Inc., 1976, p. 119.

[4] Gibran, Kahlil. *The Prophet.* New York, NY: Alfred A Knopf, 2002, p. 28. The text of this beautiful poem could have been written by a Shaker.

> *And what is it to work with love?*
> *It is to weave the cloth with thread drawn from your heart,*
> *even as if your beloved were to wear that cloth.*
> *It is to build a house with affection, even as if your beloved*
> *were to dwell in that house.*
> *It is to sow seeds with tenderness and reap the harvest with*
> *joy, even as if your beloved were to eat the fruit.*
> *It is to charge all things you fashion with a breath of your*
> *own spirit,*
> *And to know that all the blessed dead are standing about you*
> *and watching...*
> *Work is love made visible.*

This poem was well known and loved by the twentieth-century Canterbury Shakers and often quoted by them.

[5] Ott, *Hancock Shaker Village*, p. 25.

[6] Evans, *Autobiography of a Shaker,* p. 240.

[7] Blinn, *Record,* vol. 1, p. 178.

[8] Other inventors have also claimed the honor of inventing the circular saw, and this may well be a case of "convergent evolution," where several people, working independently, had the same idea.

[9] Blinn, *Memoriam,* p. 17.

[10] Andrews, *People Called Shakers,* p. 183.

[11] *Testimonies,* p. 264.

[12] The recipes for these and many other dishes are to be found in a variety of cookbooks, particularly *Seasoned with Grace* by Eldress Bertha Lindsay and *Shaker Cookbook: Not by Bread Alone* by Caroline Piercy.

[13] Andrews, *People Called Shakers,* p. 183.

[14] Blinn, *Memoriam,* p. 21.

[15] Grove Wright's journal, May 1846, quoted in Burns, *Shaker Cities,* p. 106.

[16] In November, 1963, when volunteers and visitors to Hancock heard the shocking news of John F. Kennedy's assassination, they gathered for an impromptu memorial service in the Round Stone Barn. Burns, *Shaker Cities,* p. 195.

[17] Sprigg, *By Shaker Hands,* p. 5.

[18] Andrews, *People Called Shakers,* p. 180.

[19] Charles Dickens, *American Notes for General Circulation,* 1842, quoted in Morse, *Shakers and the World's People,* p. 184.

[20] Evans, Frederick William. *Ann Lee (The Founder of the Shakers): A Biography.* Albany, NY: Charles van Benthuysen and Sons, 1858, p. 59.

[21] Frederick Evans to Leo Tolstoy, Mar. 6, 1891, quoted in Morse, *Shakers and the World's People,* p. 235.

Arise, O My Children

Arise, O my children, to me gather here,
I warn you of danger and trials appear,
Come gird up your loins, O my chosen prepare
Deep scenes of affliction to patiently bear.

— "Mother's Warning," 1846[1]

On a quiet autumn day, a shocking act of terrorism forever changed the United States of America. The attack, planned and executed by a small group of zealots, was brief, but its impact was immense and far-reaching; it helped to plunge the nation into war. It happened more than a century ago, and was led by a man whose simple name became a household word — John Brown.

On October 16, 1859, John Brown led a small but determined group of men on what would turn out to be a suicide mission. They attacked the federal arsenal at Harper's Ferry, Virginia. Their goal was to seize weapons and instigate an armed rebellion that would sweep across the nation and end the institution of slavery forever.

But the raid was a disaster. Slaves did not rise up against their masters and flock to join Brown's men. As soon as the raid was discovered, local militia surrounded the armory, cutting off Brown's escape routes. Shots were exchanged, and several citizens were killed. Finally, federal soldiers led by Robert E. Lee, blue-clad and leading Union troops, stormed the arsenal and captured or killed most of Brown's men.

More than a century later, the shocking events of September 11, 2001, were instant news, watched on television as they unfolded, by millions across the globe. Things moved more slowly in 1859, and the tale of John Brown spread by telegraph and railroad. Some people read the startling headlines weeks afterwards. But the nationwide impact of Harper's Ferry was not unlike that of 9/11. Both galvanized the nation into a powerful mixture of horror, confusion, patriotism, and belligerence — and the knowledge that the country would never be quite the same again.

The famous Civil War historian Bruce Catton wrote "The wind was being sown, and the hurricane would come later." Outbreaks of violence over slavery continued across the country; they were warnings of the coming tempest, "lightning flashes that set evil scarlet flares against the black clouds that were banked up along the horizon. Somewhere beyond the lightning there was thunder, and the making of a great wind that would change the face of a nation."[2]

But the thickening storm clouds were far over the horizon from the green hills of Canterbury. Henry Blinn's *Historical Record,* in which he painstakingly noted many decades of Shaker life, made no mention of the country-rocking events that were taking place in these stirring days. The Elders at New Lebanon had warned all Shakers against "partaking of any party spirit that is now existing without in relation to John Brown's invasion at Harper's Ferry."[3] Henry did not record the turmoil that was going on "without;" he wrote calmly of the Shakers' daily life: an outbreak of mumps, a debate on whether or not to raise swine, a wagon accident. He did not describe Brown's trial, an emotion-packed extravaganza which caused a sensation throughout the country.

John Brown was wildly popular in much of New England, in spite of his violent methods. Three years earlier, Brown had led an anti-slavery raid in "Bleeding Kansas," during which he and his supporters had awakened five unarmed men in the middle of the night, dragged them from their homes, and hacked them to pieces with swords. This savage act had not created much stir in the press, and to many Abolitionists, Brown was a hero and a martyr. In the North, the day of his execution was commemorated with solemn ceremonies of mourning; bells tolled and cannons fired salutes. Brown would "make the gallows as glorious as the Cross," wrote Ralph Waldo Emerson.[4]

Brown was, of course, an out-and-out villain to the pro-slavery part of the nation. The nightmare of an armed uprising by their millions of slaves had long terrified Southerners. But whether adored or detested, John Brown had undoubtedly touched a nerve. His dramatic act had forced the slavery debate to the forefront of the political scene; his violence demonstrated clearly that rational solutions were all but out of the question.

Brown himself foresaw the coming storm. Before he walked to the scaffold, on December 2, 1859, he scribbled a last message. "I John Brown am now quite *certain* that the crimes of this *guilty land: will* never be purged *away;* but with Blood."[5]

❧

During the hectic years leading up to Harper's Ferry, Henry Blinn had been immersed in the peaceful, busy world of Canterbury. A hard-working Shaker, he put his hands to many tasks, from blacksmithing to dentistry, but he found his true calling when he was set to work with children. Ironically, the celibate Shakers were surrounded by youngsters, and Henry was the parent of a family of twenty-four; he had been appointed teacher and caretaker of a group of boys aged six to sixteen.

The Shakers' attitudes towards children, like most of their convictions, were sharply at variance with the conventional ideas of the World. Children had always been of special concern to the childless Mother Ann. The outspoken leader of the Shakers was recorded as losing her temper when she encountered a woman with an ill-kempt brood of five children; Ann gave her some harsh advice. "Five!" she exclaimed. "When you had one, why did you not wait, and see if you were able to bring that up as you ought, before you had another? And when you had two, why did you not stop then?"[6]

Unlike some of the social philosophers of her day, who recommended that children were perfectly able to go out and get a job when they reached the age of six, Mother Ann insisted that children were a responsibility, not a way to augment the family income. "Are you not ashamed?" she asked the mother of the ragged children. "You must go and take up your cross, and put your hands to work, and be faithful in your business; clothe your children, and keep them clean and decent."[7] The Shakers had clothed and fed many of the World's uncared-for children ever since. But the care given to foundlings went far beyond food and clothing.

At Hancock Shaker Village, there is a small brick shed, a bit removed from the other buildings. Inside, on a long wooden seat, three well-worn oval holes reveal the shed's purpose — it's an outhouse. The building is snug and wind-proof, a rather cozy spot, and if you peer into a dark corner, now festooned with spider webs, you'll see a fourth, smaller hole placed lower down, with a handy step in front of it — just the right height for a child. All through the Shaker villages you can find child-sized things — an infant's high chair, a bucket light enough for little hands, a row of pegs conveniently set low. These were carefully and thoughtfully crafted by people who loved children.

Perhaps the childless Shaker women — and men — could value children as harassed parents with a dozen offspring could not. It became a common occurrence for families who were heading to the frontier, struggling to make ends meet, or simply didn't want another kid, to pack off extra children to the Shakers. The parents could be sure the children would receive nourishing food, warm clothes, and an education, as well as chance to learn marketable skills. Shaker villages became the first, though unofficial, orphanages in America.

Sometimes a whole family would convert, mother and father bringing the children with them to live in the new religion. Children under the age of five or so were left in their mother's care, until they were old enough to join a special Children's Order. Brothers like Henry Blinn cared for boys, while Sisters raised the girls.

Children were not denied contact with their biological parents, but were encouraged to think of themselves as members of a larger family. They became part of the village that it takes to raise a child.

Although Mother Ann had been illiterate, the Shakers came to value learning. School for the boys was held in winter, while the girls wove and spun, and learned other household skills. In summer, while the boys were working in the cropfields, it was school-time for the girls, who received an education similar to that of the boys.

Shortly after his student days ended, Henry Blinn was appointed teacher. The brand-new nineteen-year-old schoolmaster must have been nervous as he stood for the first time behind the master's desk, facing pupils only a few years younger than himself. But he took to his new job like a duck to water. Pail-making and farm-work had been duties faithfully performed, but teaching was his niche.

The young schoolmaster loved his trade. He was constantly looking for innovative ways of teaching that would enliven the mind. Originally, Shaker schools had stressed crafts and practical skills, but progressive educators like Henry opened the door to other studies. He taught the basics: reading, spelling, geography, math. But soon he introduced new, up-to-date topics of study: botany, geology, biology, physiology — he even taught anatomy, which caused a stir among conservative Shakers. "Quite a varied opinion in regard to this study, but better judgment prevailed and it held an honorable place among the school studies," Henry wrote, even adorning the walls of the classroom with anatomical illustrations.[8] It was a thoroughly up-to-date institution; the schoolhouse was a comfortable building, well-lit, heated and ventilated, equipped with books, maps, and globes.

His school was a gentle place compared with educational institutions in the World — and even with those of today, given the bedlam of shrilling bells and loudspeaker announcements that is a modern school. This was the era when "spare the rod and spoil the child" was thought to be a gospel truth. Most schoolboys, like Tom Sawyer, pretty much expected to "get a lickin'" almost every day.

But in Shaker schools, corporal punishment was forbidden; rulers were only used for measuring, not to whack small palms, and birch rods and whips were unknown. In the back of Henry's classroom was a cot, a comfortable place for a tired child to rest.

Funds were tight, and Henry kept meticulous account of all the school expenses. Paper was so precious it was used only on special occasions. But one year he set aside the sum of $1.00 for "peppermints and candies for the children," a sizeable amount, considering that a year's supply of steel pens, costing 75 cents, was "so very expensive."[9]

Shaker scholars, like the harassed students of today, had to endure standardized testing. In 1850, a rumor that Canterbury Village had no school led to an inspection by a ten-person delegation from the New Hampshire Commission on Education. They invaded the little classroom and spent almost five hours examining the children, girls as well as boys. Henry proudly recorded that the inspectors pronounced their "very general satisfaction."[10]

Henry also served as caretaker of the boys before and after school hours, providing maternal care to youngsters from kindergarten to high-school age, "with the thousand and one little wants to be met." He was happy and fulfilled in parenting his flock, and "enjoyed a home in the midst of a large and busy family."[11]

But after a decade of contented service, an unwelcome change came to him. He wrote sadly, "It was a great cross to leave the children."[12] But already the ranks of the Canterbury Brethren were thinning, and his abilities were needed for more challenging tasks. He saw his duty clearly when he was called to serve. In 1852, this talented and articulate man was made an Elder, at the ripe old age of twenty-eight.

∽

As Elder, Henry Blinn was concerned with the doings of the Believers, but not with those of the World. Only a few selected Shakers had business dealings with outsiders; the rest were not expected to interest themselves in the World's events — especially in the arena of politics.

Most Americans, however, were following politics with passionate interest. Before the days of professional sports, even local elections could spark the same frenzied ardor that today is inspired by the Superbowl. The issue of slavery had electrified the nation, so that the presidential campaign of 1860 was an especially fierce one, which everyone knew would have immense consequences. On Election Day that year, there was a voter turnout of over 80%; for the hotly contested Gore-Bush election of 2000, the turnout was 54%.

Henry Blinn did not cast his ballot for Stephen Douglas, John Breckinridge, John Bell, or Abraham Lincoln, although Henry, like many New Englanders, was wholeheartedly in favor of abolition. Darryl Thompson, a Shaker scholar who grew up with the last Shaker Sisters at Canterbury, recalls "As a child, I heard Sister Lillian Phelps of Canterbury tell a story. She said that during the election of 1860 the Canterbury Shaker Brethren were asked where they stood. One replied, 'We don't vote, but we are all Lincoln men.'"[13]

No matter what their personal beliefs, Shakers did not vote at all. And, of course, neither women nor African-Americans yet had the right to vote. But there were enough "Lincoln men" to carry the day. Abraham Lincoln won the election, on November 6, 1860, although with less than 40% of the popular vote. He carried every Northern state except New Jersey, but his name did not even appear on the ballot in many Southern states.

As the 1860s opened, Elder Henry's *Historical Record* recounted only the details of agricultural life: "3,068 lbs. of cheese made, 1895 yds. cloth woven, 128 gall. apple sauce."[14] The big communal farm at Canterbury was thriving. "We have builded a sheep barn. Have repaired the carding mill and put in a new water wheel."[15]

South Carolina seceded from the Union on December 20, 1860, only weeks after Lincoln's election. The terrible threat of war was growing closer. As the new year rolled in, Henry may have felt like a man acknowledging the symptoms of a terrible disease which can no longer be denied. He wrote, "Jan. 4, 1861: A national fast is proclaimed by the president of the U.S. to avert, if possible, the spirit of rebellion which seems to be growing in the country."[16] The president he referred to was the lame duck James Buchanan, since presidents were then inaugurated in March, not January. President-elect Lincoln was still waiting in Springfield, Illinois.

Events were moving swiftly. In January, 1861, Mississippi, Florida, Alabama, Georgia, and Louisiana all seceded, and Texas followed suit in February. The new president was inaugurated in March, and Abraham Lincoln became the commander-in-chief of a nation that was tearing itself apart. The dark clouds of war were no longer far away on the horizon; the storm was beginning to break.

Cannonballs flew at Fort Sumter in April, after which four more Southern states left the Union. Battle soon followed with the startling Confederate victory at Bull Run in July. The first casualty lists were printed; the first war widows began to wear the black clothes of mourning.

But the year 1861 was an uneventful one at Canterbury. The seasons went by as ever: March was maple-sugaring, spring was the time for plowing and planting, hay-making came in June. In July, Henry mentioned, a little wearily, that the "great barns are whitewashed, twice;" perhaps he wielded a brush himself.[17]

It wasn't till December that he referred again to the terrible events in the outside world, in which the inhabitants seemed to have gone insane. "This year we have kept two National fasts, to pray for the welfare of the country, which is involved in all the horrors of a civil war."[18]

Notes

[1] Cohen, *Simple Gifts*, p. 48.

[2] Catton, Bruce. *This Hallowed Ground: The Union Side of the Civil War.* Garden City, NY: Doubleday and Company, Inc., 1955, p. 10.

[3] Stein, *Shaker Experience*, p. 201.

[4] Klein, Maury. *Days of Defiance: Sumter, Secession and the Coming of the Civil War.* New York, NY: Alfred A. Knopf, Inc., 1997, p. 59.

[5] Lankford, Nelson. *Cry Havoc! The Crooked Road to the Civil War, 1861.* New York, NY: Viking Press, p. 4.

[6] *Testimonies,* p. 313.

[7] Ibid.

[8] Blinn, *Record,* vol. 1, p. 168.

[9] Ibid., p. 164.

[10] Ibid., p. 167.

[11] Blinn, *Memoriam,* p. 32.

[12] Ibid., p. 31.

[13] Darryl Thompson, personal communication, October, 2008.

[14] Blinn, *Record,* vol. 1, p. 179.

[15] Ibid., p. 178.

[16] Ibid., p. 180.

[17] Ibid., p. 181.

[18] Ibid., p. 182.

A Fire Bell in the Night

*This momentous question, [of slavery] like a fire bell in
the night, awakened and filled me with terror. I considered
it at once as the death knell of the Union.*

— Thomas Jefferson[1]

To the Shakers, perhaps the most terrifying sound in the world
was an alarm-bell clanging in the night. Nothing was more fearful
than awakening to a sky filled with red glare, the crackle of flames,
and the choking smell of smoke. Time after time, many of their finest buildings were devastated by fire.

In a world lit by candles and lanterns, and heated by wood
or coal, the risk of fire was always present. But the Shakers, with
their enormous buildings housing a hundred or more people, were
especially at risk. The giant barns, stuffed with tons of tinder-
dry hay, were particularly vulnerable. A single spark could mean
disaster.

The Shakers exercised their considerable ingenuity to avoid
fires. Barn floors were sometimes built without nails, so that no
sparks could be struck by an iron-shod wagon wheel. Hay-mows
were well-lighted with broad windows, so that there was less need
for lanterns. Sand boxes and water buckets were kept handy to put
out any stray sparks, and the Millennial Laws included rules for
fire prevention. Still the Shakers dreaded the sound of the fire-bell,
calling them out of bed to the hopeless task of extinguishing an
inferno with buckets of water.

But no precautions, no ingenuity, could avert the fire that was now raging in the World. The violence ignited by John Brown had engulfed the nation. 1861 had been followed by an even more dreadful year.

"No soldier who took part in the two day's engagement at Shiloh ever spoiled for a fight again," wrote one Union veteran.[2] In the spring of 1862, the Battle of Shiloh became the bloodiest battle in United States history, although it soon lost that distinction. More soldiers were killed or wounded in this one battle than in the American Revolution, the War of 1812, and the Mexican-American War — combined.

The Civil War was extraordinarily bloody because battlefield tactics had not caught up with advances in weaponry. Here was a use for technology that the Shakers had not considered; improved weapons were capable of killing large numbers of people with appalling efficiency. But the old-style methods of attack, from Napoleonic times and before, were still being used by unimaginative generals. Long lines of men charged across open fields, where they were mowed down wholesale.

Shiloh was followed by a long summer of hard-fought and costly battles. Then came the Battle of Antietam in September, still the bloodiest single-day battle in American history, with an estimated 23,000 casualties. The Battle of Fredericksburg in December was the crescendo of that violent year. If Henry Blinn read the newspaper accounts, he must have been aghast.

Fredericksburg was an unmitigated disaster for the North. Thirty thousand Union soldiers were ordered to assault a towering ridge called Marye's Heights, where the Confederates waited, well protected behind chest-high stone walls. Time after time, Union General Burnside ordered waves of troops to cross open ground and assault the heights under a deadly fire.

The Confederates also had massed artillery high on the bluff. Confederate Colonel E. P. Alexander watched as the blue-clad soldiers were "raked as with a fine-tooth comb" by his cannons. "A chicken could not live on that field," he remarked grimly.[3] After the battle, thousands of Union soldiers were interred in hastily-dug graves; the bodies, many unidentified, were buried in batches, sometimes six in one plot.

Henry Blinn had been horribly right when he referred to the war's battlefields as "the slaughter pen of the nation." No one had expected, no one had dreamed, that this war would last so long, or be so ghastly in its horrors, so costly in human suffering. And all this blood was being poured out, and all these men were dying — some of them, at least — over an issue that the Shakers had decided for themselves a long time ago.

〜

The Shakers, true to form, were centuries ahead of their time on the issue of civil rights. Their attitude of tolerance dated back to the maternal Ann Lee, who apparently was readier than most people of her day to accept all souls as God's children. She maintained excellent relations with the Iroquois at Niskeyuna, and Shakers ever since had lived on good terms with Native Americans. Ann Lee converted at least one "Indian woman," and several other Native American Shakers are mentioned in the records.[4]

Shakers were often viewed with suspicion for their tolerance. At Union Village, Ohio, angry neighbors accused the Believers of "endeavoring to incite the Indians against the whites . . . a charge which probably had its only foundation in the fact that large numbers of half-starving Indians had encamped at Union Village and been supplied with food by the Shakers."[5]

Henry Blinn noted, with interest and approval, that in 1860, "Two little Indian boys, Albert and Lorenzo Randolph, were received from Boston . . . [and were] admitted to this family."[6] This was a decade before US Army General Philip Sheridan expressed the feelings of most Americans when he declared, "The only good Indian is a dead Indian."[7]

〜

It's difficult to assess precisely how many African-American Shakers there were, since Shaker diaries and records do not always distinguish between blacks and whites — a mark of how truly "color-blind" Shakers could be. Violet Bennet, a black woman, joined the Shakers in the 1780s. There are records of black Brothers and Sisters at Hancock, Canterbury, New Lebanon, and many other villages.[8] Rebecca Cox Jackson, a free black woman who was a visionary preacher, lived with the Shakers at Watervliet for several years, and helped to found an urban group of Sisters, mostly black, in Philadelphia.

Mother Ann is reported as having had a vision in which she saw the "negroes, who are so much despised, redeemed from their loss, with crowns on their heads."[9] Not all Shakers were equally enlightened, of course, and probably not all Shakers welcomed African-Americans as equals. Folk who became Shakers brought their prejudices with them, especially the converts who joined as adults. The issue of race relations was most strained in the southernmost Shaker villages, Pleasant Hill and South Union, both located in the slave-holding state of Kentucky. It wasn't until 1817 that the Shakers formally freed the slaves belonging to members in the southern societies — still nearly half a century ahead of the rest of the nation.

When a person joined the Shakers, he or she consecrated their personal property to the church — furniture, wagons, cattle, farm equipment; in the South, the property list might well include slaves. But Shaker policy, from the beginning, regarded blacks as human souls, not chattels. If the slave-owner decided to abandon Shakerism and return to the World, his slaves were allowed to remain if they wished to. This sometimes caused controversy between Shakers and slave-masters, and on more than one occasion the Shakers came up with the funds to buy the freedom of a slave. Some former slaves converted and joined as Brothers and Sisters; others remained as paid workers. African-Americans were considered full-fledged Shakers in most villages (Figure 7). Only at South Union, Kentucky, was there a "Black Family" that lived apart, with a black Elder who was a former slave named Neptune.

Figure 7. In this contemporary engraving, a black Shaker dances in line with other Brethren. Use courtesy of The Granger Collection, New York, NY.

But the Shakers, however progressive their treatment of minorities, did not take a formal stand on abolition. They stubbornly clung to their practice of abstaining from the World's politics — and there was no hotter political issue than slavery.

Some Shakers spoke out with forthright courage, nonetheless. Eldress Paulina Bates of Watervliet, New York, wrote passionately about the abomination of slavery, and she doubtless expressed the feelings of many Shakers. But down south, Shakers were surrounded by violently pro-slavery sentiment. Some Kentucky Shakers made a point of tactfully avoiding discussion of the subject with their slave-owning neighbors, so as not to arouse controversy and ill-feeling.[10]

The Shakers made their opinions known in subtle ways. Many Abolitionists avoided the use of white sugar, since the slaves on sugar plantations toiled in especially brutal and wretched conditions. Maple sugar was a good alternative. "Make your own sugar and send not to the Indies for it," recommended an article in the Farmers' Almanac, as early as 1803. "Feast not on the toil, pain, and misery of the wretched."[11] This is perhaps the earliest example of socially responsible consumerism, the precursor of today's products like "Fair Trade" coffee, which is grown by Third World farmers guaranteed a fair price for their product, or "chocolate with a conscience," which is not gathered or processed with the use of child labor. Shakers in northern villages developed a gigantic maple sugar industry, tapping tens of thousands of trees annually.

Though no longer owners of slaves themselves, Shakers, at least the southern ones, must have often been first-hand witnesses of the realities of slavery. In 1831, a South Union blacksmith was hired to do ironwork for a non-Shaker who lived nearby; the Shaker smith repaired plows and horseshoes, mended pots and bridles. He also, as requested, made a "new tress for Black man" and forged a large "Chain link."[12]

Henry himself had no doubt at all where he stood on the question of buying and selling human beings. As a boy in Providence, among the first books he spelled over were anti-slavery booklets, presented by "kind-hearted men from the Anti-Slavery society office," and these books had a strong influence on the child. "From these tracts came the first impressions to my mind of the wrongs and cruelty of slavery, and years have only increased the intensity of these first lessons."[13]

It is uncertain how much of a part the Shakers played in the Underground Railroad. The journal of the South Family at Watervliet, New York, for instance, contains several references to fugitive slaves, but with a tantalizing lack of detail. "June 28, 1848: George to Schenectady to take Mary, a black runaway slave."[14] "Oct. 3, 1859: James F. to Albany with a runaway Negro to help him on to Canada."[15] Many individual Shakers obviously sympathized with the cause of abolition. But no firm evidence for a Shaker village as an established Underground Railroad station has so far been discovered.

An early Shaker leader had mused on the evils that God so inexplicably allows to thrive. At a loss to explain the suffering he had seen, he sadly wrote "How to account for it, we are unable, only that God seeth not as Man seeth, and when ever he feels to chastise his people he sees and knows what is for their good."[16]

This attitude may have been frustrating for those Shakers who felt that God helps those who help themselves. As Elder Grove Wright put it, "A good many Christians pray that the world may be converted and then sit down and wait for God to answer their prayers. But if they are farmers, they never pray that God will plough their corn fields, and then get up on the fence and wait to see the dirt fly."[17]

At some villages, there were those who grew restless, and enlisted. A crowd of young recruits "left Pittsfield at 8 A.M. this (Wednesday) morning," a Massachusetts newspaper noted in 1861. They were off to join the Twenty-First Regiment of Massachusetts Volunteers. "Among the number was a young Shaker boy, and a wagon-load of the brethren and sisters were at the Depot to see him off."[18]

Not all Shakers were on the side of the Union. At Pleasant Hill, some young Brothers were enticed by the columns of Confederate soldiers marching past, and decided to join up. Most of the Brethren were doubtless more accustomed to handling hoes than rifles, and Brother Thomas Chaplin accidently shot himself in the foot as he prepared to join the army.[19]

But other Shakers, and most importantly the Shaker leadership, took a different view of the question of enlistment. The Central Ministry at New Lebanon made their position clear; the Elders wrote to Canterbury to state unequivocally: "<u>Believers,</u> who are <u>obeyers,</u> cannot, under any circumstances, engage in military servitude of any <u>name</u> or <u>nature</u>!"[20]

Going to war to kill other people was out of the question for Believers, no matter what the rest of the country did. It was not "possible to convince us that we could love a man and shoot him at the same time," Elder Harvey Eads of South Union pointed out firmly.[21] "So that, according to Shaker doctrines, there can be no such thing as a *Christian* warrior," wrote Elder Frederick Evans. "The time has come to beat the sword into a plowshare, and the spear into a pruning hook, and . . . not practice or learn war any more."[22]

Notes

[1] Jefferson, Thomas. *The Life and Selected Writings of Thomas Jefferson,* edited by Adrienne Koch and William Peden. New York, NY: Random House, Inc., 1944, p. 698.

[2] *http://www.nps.gov/shil,* a National Park Service website.

[3] *http://www.civilwarhome.com.*

[4] Patterson, *Shaker Spiritual,* p. 352.

[5] *The History of Warren County, Ohio.* Chicago, IL: W. H. Beers and Co., 1882, p. 442. Available at *http://www.rootsweb.ancestry.com/~ohwarren/,* the website of OHGenWeb, a non-profit organization whose goal is to provide online Ohio historical and genealogical information to the public.

[6] Blinn, *Record,* vol. 1, p. 177.

[7] Some sources state that Sheridan actually said, "The only good Indians I ever saw were dead." No matter how he worded it, the sentiment was a popular one, and the remark became a proverb.

[8] Williams, Richard E. *Called and Chosen; the Story of Mother Rebecca Jackson and the Philadelphia Shakers.* Metuchen, NJ: The Scarecrow Press, Inc., and The American Theological Library Association, 1981, p. 147.

[9] *Testimonies,* p. 43.

[10] White and Taylor, *Shakerism,* p. 179.

[11] Burns, *Shaker Cities,* p. 60.

[12] Stein, *Shaker Experience,* p. 139.

[13] Blinn, *Memoriam,* p. 9.

[14] *Records of the South Family of the United Society, called Shakers, in the town of Watervliet, Albany County and State of New York, July 4, 1830–December 13, 1887.* In the collection of the Shaker Heritage Society, Albany, NY, p. 17.

[15] Ibid., p. 22.

[16] Burns, *Shaker Cities,* p. 56.

[17] *The Shaker Manifesto,* vol. 10, no. 3, March 1880, p. 71.

[18] *Pittsfield Sun,* August 29, 1861.

[19] Clark, *Pleasant Hill in the Civil War,* p. 32.

[20] New Lebanon Ministry to Canterbury Ministry, July 19, 1863. In the collection of the Shaker Museum and Library, Old Chatham, NY.

[21] White and Taylor, *Shakerism,* p. 197.

[22] Evans, *Ann Lee,* p. 62.

Sitting on a Volcano

Dark is the cloud that rests over the nation,
Wild is the war cry that pierces the air,
God's heavy judgments spread wide desolation,
Strong hearts are bowed in the depths of despair.

— Shaker hymn, 1862[1]

In 1863, the year Henry Blinn was drafted, Canterbury Village had hosted "a missionary by the name of Smith" who came for a visit and "brought with him some Hindoo gods." Henry was intrigued and noted, "The interview was very interesting."[2] The Shakers might have been surprised as well as interested to find that pacifism, one of their most basic tenets, was not a Christian monopoly.

Far back into history, individuals and societies have made the decision to abstain from war. Ancient Hindu doctrines espoused "ahimsa," a doctrine of non-violence, more than two thousand years ago. Other religions more ancient than Christianity, such as Buddhism, taught pacifism as well. The idea that the moral person should not participate in war did not originate with Jesus.

The Christian tradition was, if anything, maddeningly ambiguous. Jesus told Peter, "Put up again thy sword into his place: for all they that take the sword shall perish with the sword."[3] But in 312 CE, a pagan Roman Emperor, the belligerent Constantine, claimed to have had a vision from heaven on the eve of battle; he placed the symbol of Christ on his soldiers' shields, and assured his men that this meant victory. Whether his vision was divine inspiration or shrewd propaganda, Constantine won a resounding and crucial victory against an army twice the size of his own. Christianity was on its way to becoming a mainstream religion, sanctioned by the state.

The peaceful words of Jesus became the gospel of Christ, the official religion throughout Rome, then Europe. But pacifism was an inconvenient way to maintain a government. Rulers frequently found it expedient to overlook the parts of the Bible that advocated non-violence. Over the centuries, officials of the Church — the representatives of Christ — sanctioned wars, blessed wars, and, on occasion, enthusiastically participated in wars.

As the Reformation developed, some Protestant groups, such as the Quakers and the Mennonites, re-examined the teachings of Jesus, and embraced non-violence as a basic principle, insisting that war was contrary to Christian morality. Shakers had adopted this idea when the Shaking Quakers had splintered off from mainstream Quakerism.

Mother Ann freely expressed her opinions on pacifism. During the American Revolution, she faced down a military man, General James Sullivan, who was seeking to coerce male Shakers into military service. "I want men to go and fight for the country," he told her bluntly.

Perhaps deliberately echoing the words of Jesus, Mother Ann replied: "You never will kill the Devil with a sword."[4]

From the American Revolution through the War of 1812, Shakers petitioned state governments for exemption whenever a militia draft was called. Sometimes, Brothers could buy their freedom from "military servitude." While Joseph Meacham stated that "we cannot, consistent with our faith and conscience, bear the arms of war," he did suggest, somewhat uncertainly, that "if they require, by fines or taxes of us . . . we may, *for peace sake,* answer their demands in that respect and be innocent so far as we know at present."[5] Over the years, Shakers paid thousands of dollars in "muster fines."

But the War of 1812 was a costly and unpopular war that slowly dragged to an inconclusive halt. The peace treaty of 1814 returned virtually all conditions to the "*status quo ante bellum*" — back to the way they had been before the shooting began.[6] Perhaps it was this reminder of the futility of war that convinced the Shakers that they could no longer participate, even if only by paying fines that aided other men to fight.

In 1815, the Shaker leadership at New Lebanon published a declaration that stated "We feel ourselves impelled by the most sacred obligations of duty, to decline rendering our personal services, hiring substitutes, paying an equivalent, or doing any thing whatever to aid, or abet the cause of war, let the consequences be what they may." To do so, they stated flatly, would be to admit that liberty of conscience "may be purchased of government at a stated price."[7]

Their declaration of independence from the nation's wars was a polite document, which included the assurance "Nay, we sincerely respect the government." It courteously explained the Shaker point of view, and pointed out that Believers willingly fulfilled all other civic obligations. But the Shakers were as unyielding as Patrick Henry when they declared "liberty of conscience more dear to us than life itself."[8]

The drafting of soldiers was still at this time a matter for individual states, not the federal government. So, for many Shaker villages, the question was moot. In Massachusetts and New Hampshire, state law granted the right of conscientious objection.[9] Maine and Connecticut had special exemptions for the Shakers and other pacifists written into their constitutions.

But some states, notably New York, firmly disagreed with the Shakers' stand, and took legal action. Dozens of Shakers were court-martialled or jailed. Many New York Brethren solved the problem by leaving home whenever the draft loomed, and resettling in Hancock, only a few miles over the Massachusetts border. This became so common that the efficient Hancock Shakers took to providing pre-printed proof-of-residence forms for the newly arrived Brothers.[10]

However, as the twentieth-century anti-war activist Ammon Hennacy remarked, "Being a pacifist between wars is as easy as being a vegetarian between meals." Legal wrangles over the Shakers' status dragged on in the courts, but the penalties for refusing military service were not generally taken very seriously. Jailed Shakers were released after short terms, and the fines were sometimes waived. The issue in New York and other states was never conclusively decided. During the period of relative calm and prosperity that followed the War of 1812, the issue was on the back burner. No one really cared too much if the eccentric Shakers objected to war — when there were no wars to fight.

But in 1861, everything changed, as the nation advanced enthusiastically to battle. Now the question of the Shakers' military status became a very hot issue indeed — for the state authorities, and for the Shakers themselves.

Both the North and the South, in the inevitable habit of armies, confidently claimed that God was on their side. This kind of "Onward, Christian Soldiers" mentality was not unfamiliar to the Shakers, who sometimes saw themselves as warriors for the Gospel. Some of their songs had very belligerent lyrics: "I will fight fight & never slack . . . fight & slay the enemy."[11] The enemy they battled, however, was sin: the Devil, who they sometimes referred to as "Old Stiff."

But the Civil War was a conflict that was brutally real. The war was coming closer and closer to home, and many Shakers viewed the situation with gathering dread. The Kentucky villages, especially, were right in the thick of things. A Pleasant Hill Shaker wrote in disgust, as soldiers passed right through his village: "[The soldiers] are training & drilling & trying to learn the most successful methods of letting out the heart's blood of their opponents, brother against brother, and father & son against each other. And for what! It is a doubtful question whether any of them on either side are able to tell what they are furiously seeking the lives of each other like demons for."[12]

Hard questions were before all Shakers now, unavoidable and frightening. Henry Blinn, and the other Brothers of draftable age must have wrestled with their consciences — as did Abraham

Lincoln — as millions have done before and since. *Is there such a thing as a "just" war? Could I kill another human being? Shall I do evil, in order to right a greater evil?*

For the Brothers who were beyond the age of conscription, and the Sisters, the questions were less personal but no less difficult. The Central Ministry, the Shakers' governing body, had to decide the issue once and for all, as did all Shakers in their own hearts: should Shakers participate in the World's wars?

The Shakers had decided, early on, to withdraw from the World, but the World had withdrawn from them as well. The Believers had been eyed with deep suspicion since that hot August day in 1774 when Mother Ann and her little group first got off the boat. One Massachusetts town went so far as to pass laws prohibiting local millers to grind Shaker grain, and forbidding blacksmiths to shoe Shaker horses.[13] Many living Shakers still remembered the days of persecution: mockery, beatings, jailings, and torch-bearing mobs threatening to burn their barns and homes. Some Shakers must have felt that they were under no obligation to help the World straighten out its problems.

But the World was now willing to count the Shakers among its numbers. By the 1860s, anti-Shaker feeling had largely subsided. Except for a few annoyed parents trying to persuade rebellious youngsters to return home, or apostates suing to recover their worldly goods, Shakers were pretty much taken for granted, and often regarded with the tolerant amusement with which we view the Amish today.

The Shaker seed peddler, a gentle, straw-hatted figure driving a wagon packed with vegetable and flower seeds, was a familiar part of the rural landscape. Shaker goods were on the shelves of stores — everyone bought Shaker applesauce, baskets, chairs, herbal medicines. In spite of their determination to withdraw from the World, the Shakers had become a part of it, bound to their neighbors by a web of obligations, commerce, and laws. And to Uncle

Sam, there seemed no reason why healthy young Shaker men should be exempted from the duties of citizens.

When the Civil War began, in the bright and optimistic spring of 1861, conscription was unnecessary — the very thought was laughably unpatriotic. But as the war dragged on, the states were required to field more and more men. Militia draftees began to grumble, then to protest. Riots broke out in state after state: Pennsylvania, Wisconsin, Ohio, Indiana. Angry mobs injured draft officials; in Indiana, two were killed.[14]

In the fall of 1862, Lincoln issued a proclamation which suspended the right of habeas corpus and authorized the arrest of any person guilty of "any disloyal practice."[15] Draft resisters were subject to martial law, and hundreds were jailed without trial or due process.

In the dismal spring of 1863, the Union had come perilously close to losing the war. There was talk in the North of making peace overtures to the Confederacy. Recruitment for the Union Army was at an all-time low. In March, President Lincoln signed one of the most unpopular laws ever passed by the United States Congress — the Conscription Act.

Previously, Union soldiers had been drafted by their home states. The Conscription Act was the first wartime draft of United States citizens for national military service.[16] Men between the ages of 20 and 35, and unmarried men up to 45, were eligible to be drafted for a period of three years. Henry Blinn was thirty-eight years old, so that, had he been a married man, he would have been exempt.

A provision added that a fee of $300 could be paid instead of serving. This was a shockingly large amount — previous muster fines had been in the range of $4 — and the enormous sum was far beyond the reach of many men, especially the recent flood of Irish immigrants, who might not see so much money in a year's work. Angry folk muttered that it was a "rich man's war and a poor man's fight."

❧

July, 1863, was perhaps not the ideal time to begin the first national draft. It was only days after the publication of staggering casualty lists from the three-day battle at Gettysburg — an estimated total of 50,000 killed, wounded, and missing on both sides. A drawing for the draft was held in New York City, triggering an explosion of hatred and violence that Abraham Lincoln later described as "a volcano."[17]

It began like a scene from the Vietnam era. A mob of unwilling potential draftees, thousands strong, marched in the streets carrying placards painted with the words "NO DRAFT." The protest soon erupted into savage violence that raged for almost a week. Telephone poles were cut down, train tracks ripped up, buildings set aflame. Rioters battled with the police at first, then the wrath of the mob turned to the city's black population, choosing them as scapegoats for the unpopular war. African-Americans became the targets of ghastly brutalities.

A black man was beaten, lynched, and set on fire by a cheering mob. The rioters stormed the Colored Orphan Asylum, threatening to murder the children; the building was burned to the ground as the terrified orphans fled. Hundreds of black New Yorkers were beaten, drowned, or hanged. Thousands were driven from their homes.

The municipal police were totally unable to control the riot. Military help was not available, as the New York State militia had been sent off to help counter Robert E. Lee's invasion of Pennsylvania, and the army was still dealing with the aftermath of Gettysburg. Days of chaos passed before troops could arrive.

Finally, the violence ebbed away. The charred skeletons of buildings gave New York City the air of a battlefield. More than a hundred people died (the body count is still debated) and the damage was well over a million dollars. A modern-day historian calls the draft riots in New York City "the deadliest in American history."[18]

Abraham Lincoln was deeply shaken by what seemed to be the outbreak of another civil war. The Union appeared to be shattering. Confederates, reading of the riot in newspapers, were jubilant. Lincoln decided not to fan the flames by conducting a formal investigation into the affair.

"You have heard of sitting on a volcano," he said ruefully to a friend. "We are sitting upon two; one is blazing away already, and the other will blaze away the moment we scrape a little loose dirt from the top of the crater. One rebellion at a time is about as much as we can conveniently handle."[19]

The violence that had rocked New York City flared up in other cities as well. The conscription process continued during the hot summer months, in an atmosphere thick with bitterness and resentment, amid crowds teetering on the brink of riot.

Another round of draft notices were sent out in August, 1863. One of these informed Henry Blinn that he was "legally drafted into the service of the United States for the period of Three years," in accordance with the provisions of the act of Congress, "for enrolling and calling out the national forces."[20]

Notes

[1] Patterson, *Shaker Spiritual*, p. 436. Sister Cecelia De Vere is recorded as having received this in a dream in 1862. Different sources give her last name as De Vere, Devyr, or Devere.

[2] Blinn, *Record*, vol. 1, p. 187.

[3] *Holy Bible*, Matthew 26:52.

[4] *Testimonies*, p. 315.

[5] Andrews, Edward Deming, and Faith Andrews. *Work and Worship Among the Shakers: Their Craftsmanship and Economic Order.* New York, NY: Dover Publications, 1982, p. 163.

[6] Coles, *War of 1812*, p. 255.

[7] Schlissel, Lillian. *Conscience in America: A Documentary History of Conscientious Objection in America, 1757 to 1967.* New York, NY: E. P. Dutton and Co., Inc., 1968, p. 77.

[8] Ibid.

[9] Dickinson, *Laws of Massachusetts*, p. 82. Massachusetts law since 1810 had exempted "ferrymen . . . mariners . . . justices of the peace . . . all officers and students of any college . . . ministers of the gospel, of every denomination . . . every person of the religious denominations of Quakers and Shakers, who shall, on or before the first Tuesday of May annually, produce a certificate to the commanding office for the company, within whose bounds such Quaker or Shaker resides; which certificate, signed by two or more of the elders or overseers, as the case may be, and countersigned by the clerk of the society with which such Quaker or Shaker meets for religious worship, shall be in substance as is herein prescribed."

The certificate was a simple form that had to be filled out:

We, the subscribers, of the society of the people called_____ , in the town of _____ , in the county of _____ , do hereby certify that _____ is a member of our Society, and that he frequently and usually attends with said Society for religious worship, and we believe is conscientiously scrupulous of bearing arms. Dickinson, *Laws of Massachusetts*, p. 271.

[10] Burns, *Shaker Cities*, p. 87.

[11] Patterson, *Shaker Spiritual*, p. 334. This song was received at South Union in 1842.

[12] Clark, *Pleasant Hill in the Civil War*, p. 23.

[13] Burns, *Shaker Cities*, p. 26.

[14] Schecter, *Devil's Work*, p. 86.

[15] Donald, *Lincoln*, p. 380.

[16] In 1792, Congress had passed a Militia Act requiring, among other things, that every able-bodied white male between the ages of 18 and 45 join their local militia. It exempted various persons, including members of Congress, ferry-men, mariners, and all persons who were exempted by the laws of their state. The Militia Act was signed by President George Washington.

The Confederacy had instituted a centralized draft in April, 1862, but Shaker villages were all in Union states. There was a "shadow" Confederate government in Kentucky for a time, and many Kentuckians, including some Shakers, had Southern sympathies.

[17] Gilmore, *Personal Recollections of Abraham Lincoln*, p. 99.

[18] Schecter, *Devil's Work*, p. 251.

[19] Gilmore, *Personal Recollections of Abraham Lincoln*, p. 99.

[20] Blinn, *Record*, vol. 1, p. 298.

"Open Wide!"

Enrolment & Draft.

No 166   Requisition for Transportation of drafted men.
Concord, N.H.
August 21, 1863.

To Supt.
Boston, Concord & Montreal Rail Road

Please furnish transportation to Henry C. Blinn, from
Canterbury to Concord. On United States Government
Service.

Anthony Colby
Provost Marshal.[1]

On the day appointed for his conscription examination, Henry Blinn dutifully set out for the mustering place at Concord. It was a September morning, and the first gold of autumn touched the maple leaves that rustled overhead. It was twenty-five years, almost to the day, since his spiritual pilgrimage had brought him to Canterbury. He must have wondered, as he walked down the familiar path, what this journey might bring.

He was not alone; three other Brothers — William Libby, A. J. Thompson, and J. S. Wright, Jr. — had received their notices, too.[2] As the little group of plainly-dressed Shakers left their sacred hill, they must have felt they were indeed leaving Holy Ground. They made their way to the small nearby town, also named Canterbury, and at the little rural train station they embarked on the

Boston, Concord, and Montreal Railroad, heading for the city of Concord, New Hampshire.

All over the North, men were reporting for duty. For those who ignored the summons, penalties could be harsh. Some states offered a cash reward for "the Arrest and delivery of Drafted Men who have failed to Report."[3] The office of Provost Marshal was created at the same time as the new draft law, and was essentially the police department of the army, to enforce laws and maintain civil order. They had broad powers to search homes, and sometimes did house-to-house checks to register men for conscription. They could detain citizens without warrant, and could arrest and imprison those who did not show up for the draft.

"You will accordingly report, on the 16th of September, at the place of rendezvous in Concord, N.H.," Henry's draft notice had stated, "or be deemed a deserter, and be subject to the penalty prescribed therefor by the Rules and Articles of War."[4]

The penalties for desertion varied. In the early days of the war, deserters were generally imprisoned, for terms ranging from days to months. But as the war dragged on, and hundreds, then thousands of men began to desert, the penalties grew stiffer: hard labor; being fettered with ball and chain; some deserters were branded with a hot iron, the letter "D" three inches high burned into their skin. Scores of deserters, on both sides, were executed by firing squad.[5]

This was not the first time Henry had traveled since he had become a Shaker, as Elders frequently went from village to village on administrative affairs. In the last few years Henry had journeyed to instruct others in the skills of dentistry, "which has become quite a business." He visited villages in Connecticut and Massachusetts "to assist about making some artificial teeth."[6] So the clanking train and the crowded passenger car were familiar to him.

But the events that occurred when they arrived at their destination were shockingly unfamiliar. Concord was only a few miles southwest of Canterbury, but it was a world away from his usual life. Henry remembered every detail of that day, which he recorded at length in his usually laconic journal; his memoirs, written decades later, show that the experience had remained vividly alive in his mind.

Concord was a railroad hub, and the station was loud with trains clanging and puffing through in clouds of dense black smoke. The gold-domed State House was a reminder that Concord was the state capital. Granite quarrying was big business, there was a thriving carriage-making industry, and shipping on the nearby Merrimack River. The streets were generally full of shoppers and loiterers, apprentices trotting on errands, wagons laden with goods.

The four Shakers proceeded, as instructed, to the office of Anthony Colby, the Provost Marshal. The office was crowded, and Henry and the other Shakers immediately withdrew from the "motley crowd." They stood against the wall a little way off. "The association, even here," Henry sniffed fastidiously, "was far from being congenial."[7] He had been withdrawn from the World for a quarter of a century. This sudden immersion was a shock.

Perhaps the most astonishing thing to any Shaker who ventured into the World was the dirt. The Shakers put enormous emphasis on cleanliness and order, often admonishing youngsters with Mother Ann's saying: "There is no dirt in heaven."[8] Everything in a Shaker village was expected to be scrubbed, whitewashed, sparkling clean.

For the Shakers, outward cleanliness was part of their spirituality, a sign of inward purity. "Sweep clean," Mother Ann once commanded a young woman, Hannah Goodrich, who was wielding a broom. The girl, thus addressed, at first thought she was being urged to be a better housekeeper. She replied, "I will, Mother." But Ann Lee repeated, again and again: "I say, sweep clean," and Hannah finally understood that Mother Ann was referring to "the floor of the heart."[9]

A by-product of this spiritual cleanliness was an enthusiasm for hygiene not generally shared by the rest of the world. Shakers maintained high standards of sanitation in their dwellings, kitchens, and infirmaries, and in their workshops and huge dairies. Worldly farmers poked fun at Shakers who even kept their cows clean and their barns tidy. In those days no one, not even the Shakers, as yet realized the deadly dangers of bacteria. When children died from drinking contaminated milk, no one understood the cause.[10] But the Shakers sensed, long before the American medical establishment caught on, that cleanliness was linked to health, and dirt to disease.

Standards of sanitation in the army were even lower than in the rest of the world. "There is not a man in the army, officer or private, that does not have from a battalion to a Brigade of Body lice on him," wrote one soldier.[11] An utter ignorance of the principles of hygiene led soldiers to dig latrines close to living quarters and wells, so as to be handy. Tens of thousands of soldiers died from diseases like typhoid as a result of drinking contaminated water. And army hospitals were the worst of all. "If a fellow has to [go to the] Hospital, you might as well say good bye," another soldier wrote bitterly.[12] Disease and infections felled far more soldiers than did bullets.

❧

Henry and his Shaker Brethren waited a long time in the foul, noisy corridor. After a "protracted" wait, the door finally "moved on its hinges just far enough to admit one person, and the Provost Marshal, Anthony Colby, stood guard to allow one or more to pass." The four Shakers were admitted up the stairs to the examining room. This was far from Holy Ground indeed. "To us was like being led to the sacrificial altar of some heathen idol."[13]

In the army's desperation to acquire manpower, many medical exams were less than thorough. One doctor approved an entire regiment by ordering the men to trot past him, and then proclaimed them all fit for service. Another conscript wrote "He [the doctor] would give us a thump on the chest, and if we were not floored nor showed any other signs of inconvenience, we were pronounced in good condition."[14]

The examination in Concord, however, was conducted with thoroughness and an assembly-line efficiency that must have chilled the Brethren. "The writer was ordered to back up against the wall and under the projecting beam of a square to ascertain the height," Henry recalled. "This over another officer asks the name and residence, which he finds in the book of those drafted. While this is in process another officer . . . repeats his discoveries in a loud voice, while another person writes it in a book, as follows: Henry C. Blinn, height 5 ft 10 in; eyes hazel; hair light chestnut; complection light."[15]

The examination continued relentlessly. "I was now taken to another apartment & before the examining surgeon, and sheltered from the view of others, who are in the same room by the drawing of a curtain. My first position reminded me of the man who attempted to swallow an island. While my jaws were very widely distended, he took a close view of my teeth and from the conclusions I have the idea that he thought 'Uncle Sam's hard tack,' would pass down in a pulverised condition."[16]

It must have seemed odd to this skilled dentist to have his own teeth examined so roughly. Henry was well used to peering into the mouths of others. Only a few months before, he had gone to the Shaker village at Shirley, Massachusetts, "to make some artificial teeth for Daniel Boler . . . the impression is taken at Shirley and the teeth arranged. The form is then taken to Boston to be vulcannised. We then . . . fit the plates for use." Henry added proudly, "It was a good Job."[17]

Henry had been practicing dentistry for years. Recently, perhaps as the membership of the village began to age, the Shakers had really been taking their teeth seriously. In 1860, Henry had fitted up a dentist shop, complete with padded reclining chair, and tools for filling cavities and extracting teeth. As usual, the Shakers were the first in the neighborhood to try out a new technology. "Vulcanised rubber for plate has been introduced which gives general satisfaction."[18]

Henry's teeth having been approved, the examination continued relentlessly. "Second position. Open your eyes! This was for inspection of the optic nerve . . .

"Third position. Eyes to the light. One more look and again he calls, — all right.

"Fourth position. Stand erect, with an order to be disrobed."[19]

Henry Blinn was used to Shaker ways; he was appalled by this cattle-call mentality. The Shakers often showed a deep sensitivity to human dignity, far ahead of their time — especially in a medical setting. Shaker infirmaries, like Henry's own dentist shop, were generally state-of-the-art, with numerous ingenious devices to promote the comfort and preserve the dignity of the patients. Shaker medical men and women were pioneers in the care of the physically handicapped, with inventions such as three-legged canes (the precursors of today's walkers), comfortable commodes that ensured privacy, and the reclining hospital-style bed. In the recreated Hancock infirmary, there is still a beautifully-crafted rocking cradle, adult-size, that was used to soothe elderly patients.

The casual order to strip was a shock. The Shakers saw the human body as the seat of carnal nature, and nudity was utterly taboo. Henry, a progressive educator, had introduced the study of anatomy into the Canterbury school, but he had been a Shaker since boyhood. Being asked to stand before the examiners, stark naked, was too much.

When the order to undress was given, Henry protested with a "Christian remonstrance."

The doctor, fortunately, was easygoing; he "remarked that he did not wish to hurt my feelings, but that the law required it, and proved his point by producing a pamphlet which spelled out the rules of the examination: "Conscripts shall be examined stripped."[20]

Henry was mild and soft-spoken by nature, but perhaps dealing with twenty-four boys on a daily basis had taught him firmness. He insisted. "My remonstrance . . . took effect, and a partial disrobement, satisfied the demand."

He and the other men were examined thoroughly: muscles prodded, arms inspected, chests soundly thumped. "This closed the series of examinations and a card was given to me bearing in pencil marks my name in full, my place of residence," he wrote. And on the card was "the appalling word 'Conscript.'"[21]

The Provost Marshal, however, was a humane man who sensed Henry's panic. He "very kindly asked me if I would like a furlough of a few days. Ascertaining my feelings he wrote on my card. 'Furlough till the 22nd of September.'

"I soon left the hall and passing the guards at the foot of the stairs, once more found myself inhaling a better quality of air but not a free man." Two of the other Brothers had failed the exam, but Henry and another Brother had received a "sentence to the 'slaughter pen' of the nation."[22]

The little group of Shaker Brothers headed home in a state of shock. Henry wrote, with his usual understatement, "My mind was the storehouse of multiplied thoughts." His world had been turned upside-down. "These few moments had thrown me into a new sphere of action. My only hope is in the province of God."[23]

Notes

[1] Blinn, *Record*, vol. 1, p. 299.

[2] Ibid., p. 188.

[3] Murdock, Eugene C. *One Million Men: The Civil War Draft in the North.* Worcester, MA: Heffernan Press, Inc., 1971, p. 180.

[4] Blinn, *Record*, vol. 1, p. 298.

[5] Schlissel, *Conscience in America*, p. 148. An estimated 150 Union soldiers were executed for desertion during the war, and Confederate numbers were probably comparable. This was, however, a small fraction of the total numbers of deserters.

[6] Blinn, *Record*, vol. 1, p. 176.

[7] Ibid., p. 189.

[8] *Testimonies*, p. 265.

[9] Ibid., p. 332.

[10] Piercy, Caroline. *A Shaker Cookbook: Not by Bread Alone.* New York, NY: Crown Publishers, Inc., 1953, p. 20.

[11] Ray, Delia. *Behind the Blue and Gray: The Soldier's Life in the Civil War.* New York, NY: Scholastic Inc., p. 51.

[12] Ibid., p. 53.

[13] Blinn, *Record,* vol. 1, p. 189.

[14] Ray, *Blue and Gray,* p. 50.

[15] Blinn, *Record,* vol. 1, p. 190.

[16] Ibid.

[17] Ibid., p. 183.

[18] Ibid., p. 178.

[19] Ibid., p. 191.

[20] Ibid.

[21] Ibid.

[22] Ibid., p. 192.

[23] Ibid.

Cease To Do Evil

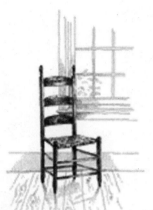

My heart is in the spirit world,
My soul is roaming there,
I dwell amid the denizens
Of that bright world so fair.

— Frederick W. Evans[1]

Tall, lean, lanky. A gaunt, weathered face with prominent cheekbones, and a trim beard. Deepset, glowing eyes. These words describe the United States' sixteenth president, Abraham Lincoln, a figure well-known to every American. They also might pass for a fair description of a less famous contemporary of Lincoln's, a Shaker Elder named Frederick Evans (Figure 8). These were the two men who would determine the fate of the drafted Shaker Brethren.

Frederick Evans was, in his way, as remarkable a person as Lincoln. They were within a few months of the same age, and both had lived rough as young men. Evans was of English birth, and sailed to America with his family when he was a boy of twelve, on a wild and stormy journey not unlike that of Mother Ann. "All hands to the pumps!" as the ship came within inches of foundering.[2]

A vigorous young man, Evans enthusiastically took to life in the New World. He farmed, got his hands dirty, learned several trades. He also, like Lincoln, was a voracious reader, devouring every book he could get his hands on. The two men must have read many of the same works: Plutarch's *Lives*, Plato's *The Republic*, Shakespeare, Voltaire, John Locke, Thomas Paine on *The Rights of*

Figure 8. Frederick Evans was a tall, spare, commanding figure, an Elder well used to guiding his flock. He was one of the Shaker Brothers who confronted Abraham Lincoln over the question of conscientious objector status for the Shakers. Use courtesy of Shaker Museum and Library, Old Chatham and New Lebanon, NY.

Man. In addition, Evans was fascinated by religion, and broad-mindedly read "the Koran and the Bibles of all peoples that I could obtain."[3] His readings left him a convinced atheist, a self-described infidel and philosopher. The young Evans had a low opinion of religion, and once proposed to found a Utopian colony, "and not to allow in it a single Christian."[4]

The idealistic young man became imbued with the ideals of "Socialistic-Communism," and determined to join a community that lived according to socialistic principles.[5] No such group being conveniently near at hand, he walked eight hundred miles, from New York to Ohio, to find one. In his autobiography, he noted that "at first, my feet swelled, and became very sore; but at length I could walk quite comfortably forty miles a day."[6]

Both of these tall, thin youngsters had a taste for travel and adventure, and they both turned to "the Father of Waters" to satisfy it. Both of them made a trip down the Mississippi by flat-boat, all the way to New Orleans — Lincoln in 1828, Evans in 1829. In the New Orleans slave market, both young men saw the brutal realities of slavery up close. The expedition "gave me an opportunity of seeing life as it existed in the then slave States," Evans wrote long after, "and I formed my own private opinion of Jefferson's remark, when he said, he 'trembled for his country, when he reflected that God was just,' which was, that he saw the end from the beginning of slavery."[7]

But after their river wanderings were over, the course of the two men's lives abruptly diverged. In 1832, Indian activity on the Illinois frontier prompted nervous officials to call for military action, and the young Abraham Lincoln joined the militia to fight in the Black Hawk War. Back east in New York State, the young Frederick Evans had joined the Shakers.

Evans, at twenty-two still on his quest for the perfect social system, paid a visit to the New Lebanon Shakers, of whom he had heard many uncomplimentary tales. He went expecting to find folk who "I supposed were the most ignorant and fanatical people in existence."[8] To the utter astonishment of his family and friends — and perhaps of himself — he became a Believer.

Evans encountered the Shakers during the peculiar period in their history known as "Mother Ann's Work." It was a time of intense spiritual revival, when many Brothers and Sisters claimed to hear voices of Mother Ann and other spirits, to see visions, and to receive gifts and revelations from another world. Some Shakers were unconvinced by the more outlandish tales of supernatural appearances, but Evans was shaken to his core.

"I was met in my own path just as the Apostle Paul was met in *his* own path," he wrote later, "by spiritual manifestations made to myself when quite alone . . . of the existence of a spirit-world."[9]

"I never have seen how I could put it into words, and do justice to the heavenly visitants," Evans wrote years later, still struggling to describe the experience that had transformed him. "One night, soon after retiring, I heard a rustling sound, as of the wind of a flock of doves flying through the window (which was closed) towards my bed . . . I was frightened, and hid my head beneath the bedclothes." Evans saw angels, lights, and the vision of "a great fire, and a nude man, perfect in his physical organism . . . he stepped into its very midst, the flames completely encircling his whole body. The next thing I observed was, that while he was perfect in *living beauty,* he was so organically changed that no "fig-leaf" covering was required."[10]

After three weeks of visions, the infidel was convinced. "I had received a revelation as truly as ever did Peter, or Paul, or Jesus, or Ann; and I therefore *believed,* not from the words of others, but . . . because I had seen, and heard, and felt, for myself."[11]

Evans became an ardent defender of Spiritualism. He often attended séances, convinced that the spirits of the dead could, and frequently did, appear and speak to the living.

In spite of his conversion, he remained deeply dedicated to challenging and reforming society, and was much more closely engaged with the World than were most Shakers. He was an outspoken advocate of women's rights and the abolition of slavery. He was a socialist who supported land reform, including the granting of free land to farmers, and laws forbidding one individual or a group of individuals to own vast holdings of land — despite the fact that in some areas it was the Shakers themselves who were the major land-holders. His motto was "Cease to do evil."

A man of wide interests, he was particularly enthusiastic about the cause of dietary reform, a subject many in those days found ridiculous. But long before the science of nutrition was born, Evans was a vegetarian who preached against the dangers of milling wheat flour superfine, thereby removing the germ and most of the vitamins. He saw clearly that ignorance of nutrition caused much suffering. Pellagra, scurvy, rickets: many deadly diseases were completely preventable by eating the proper food.

He insisted on the necessity of sanitary drinking water, in an age when germs were hardly imagined. Many thought him a crank, failing to see the insidious connection between contaminated water and disease. Abraham Lincoln's son Willie tragically died in childhood of what was called "bilious fever" but was probably typhoid contracted from contaminated Potomac River water that was piped into the White House.[12] He was one of countless children who have lost their lives to sickness caused by polluted water — a health crisis as devastating today as it was then.

Another of Evans's causes was the necessity for pure air and healthful ventilation of dwellings. Smoking disgusted him, and he authored a pamphlet titled "Twelve Reasons Why No Rational Being Should Use Tobacco." He was also opposed to the use of alcohol. Salt, he knew, can be bad for the health, but he did carry his crusade a bit far for some when he inveighed against the use of pepper and mustard, for "creating unnatural tastes and appetites."[13]

This articulate man became a renowned spokesperson for the Shakers, although his forceful opinions alienated some of his Brothers and Sisters.[14] He wrote books and articles for popular magazines about Shaker life, and hosted many prominent guests at New Lebanon. He struck up a correspondence with no less a personage than Count Leo Tolstoy. The famous Russian writer and pacifist was fascinated by the Shakers, and had many questions about their lifestyle. Evans responded by inviting him to visit New Lebanon, to see "what God hath wrought."[15] Although Tolstoy never made the trip, the two men corresponded for years.

Unlike many religious persons, Evans staunchly defended the right of others to disagree with his own beliefs. He spoke out strongly for the separation of church and state, and applauded a law that forbade the reading of the Bible in schools. When a prominent newspaper editor (and apostate Shaker) named D. M. Bennett was put on trial for sending "obscenity" through the mail, Evans sprang to his defense. The obscenity in question was a scandalously frank tract on "sexual self-government," including birth control. Bennett was an outspoken atheist who despised religion, and Frederick Evans disagreed with everything Bennett stood for.

But Evans went far out on a limb to defend Bennett. He wrote an editorial for the influential *New York Tribune* that was a ringing defense of freedom of speech. "As my soul liveth," declared Evans, "I would rather have the repeal of all laws for the suppression of vile publications than this . . . suppression of free opinion." Evans didn't mince words: "What pranks before high heaven are those that are being played in the name of religion!"[16]

At the start of the Civil War, Evans was fifty-three, a tall, spare, commanding figure, an Elder well used to guiding his flock. He realized that the War Between the States would cause enormous problems for the Shakers. Even before the federal draft laws were passed, he and other Elders and Eldresses had begun to consider the problem of conscription.

The Shakers had hard decisions to make, as the options for conscientious objectors were few. They could refuse to serve, and take the consequences of a court-martial. They could leave the country on the sly: head north to Canada, or west to Indian Territory. Or they could try to raise the sums necessary to purchase substitutes for the Brothers who were eligible for the draft: $300 a head.

But this option, chosen by so many, they utterly rejected. "It would compromise our principles less to render our services than it would to hire a substitute to do the same services for us," the Elders declared.[17] On the other hand, running and hiding would not serve, either. The Shakers wanted to establish the legal right of a conscientious objector to refuse to take part in war.

They were not planning a rebellion. Shakers took pride in being good citizens, willing to work within the system, and they professed their faith in the American way. "We believe . . . our Government will respect the principle of religious liberty . . . and we await the trial of the national honesty with calmness and confidence." However, they had experienced the World's persecutions too long not to be a little suspicious, or perhaps they were merely realistic. "If our national profession of religious toleration is all a tinsel, the sooner the deception is exposed, the better."[18]

Here, too, was a chance to show what the Shaker faith really meant. "The eyes of the nation are now upon us," the New Lebanon Elders wrote. "If we stand, like men of God . . . the Lord will help us, to come off victorious for truth, right, and the preservation of a constitutional principle, by the observance of which our nation will be blest."[19]

Hundreds of conscientious objectors from other sects had been conscripted into state militias during the past few years. Quakers, of course, were also pacifists, but Quakerism was a much more loosely organized religion than the Shakerism which had developed from it. Individual Quakers varied widely as to their stand on the war: some consented to serve, others agreed to pay the commutation fee. Some absolutely refused to fight — and had a hard time of it when they found themselves drafted into the ranks.

In both North and South, conscientious objectors could be treated with brutality. Men who refused to carry a gun were generally assumed to be unpatriotic cowards. Some were mocked by having guns tied to their backs; others were subjected to humiliations such as being hung by their thumbs, or tied spread-eagled on the ground for hours. Some were beaten, or stabbed with bayonets for refusing to bear arms. Brutal officers attempted to starve pacifists into submission, denied them water, or imprisoned them in the harsh conditions faced by all prisoners of war.[20]

∾

Sometimes, when friends or relatives could interest higher authorities in the matter, conscientious objectors were pardoned or furloughed on a case-by-case basis. Horace Taber, a Shaker Brother from Shirley, Massachusetts, was conscripted in the August 1863 draft, despite his poor health. When he did not report for duty, he was arrested and imprisoned, though not ill-treated. His health was so poor — he was "nearly blind in one eye and suffered from severe bronchitis and neuralgia" — that the Elders at Shirley were able to obtain his discharge on medical grounds after a few weeks.[21]

Sometimes requests for release went all the way up to the presidency, on both sides, with Abraham Lincoln being far more sympathetic than Jefferson Davis. But there was no clear legal avenue, and the status of pacifists was murky and bewildering. Decisions were made by different authorities in different states, and the rich or well-connected fared better than others. Conscientious objectors were being ground between the millstones of bureaucracy and indifference.

Now the fate of the conscripted Shakers hung in the balance; many more Brethren were eligible and could soon be drafted as well. With a sound military instinct, Frederick Evans and other Elders realized that the best defense is a good offense. They saw clearly that dealing with a host of subordinates and minor officials would be time-consuming. Shaker Brothers might be carted off to battle, willy-nilly, and could well be dead and buried before their case had been decided. Time was of the essence.

The spiritual children of Mother Ann were never afraid to question authority. They agreed to send a delegation direct to Washington to thrash the matter out, and they decided to go right to the top. The Shakers planned a confrontation with Abraham Lincoln.

Notes

[1] White and Taylor, *Shakerism*, p. 342. These words are recorded as part of a divinely inspired song received by Frederick Evans from spirits in a dream.

[2] Evans, Frederick William. *Autobiography of a Shaker, and Revelation of the*

Apocalypse. New York, NY: American News Co., 1888, p. 12.

[3] Ibid., p. 14.

[4] Ibid., p. 15.

[5] Ibid., p. 14.

[6] Ibid., p. 15.

[7] Ibid.

[8] Ibid., p. 16.

[9] Ibid., p. 17.

[10] Ibid., p. 20.

[11] Ibid., p. 24.

[12] Holzer, *Dear Mr. Lincoln,* p. 25.

[13] Stein, *Shaker Experience,* p. 306.

[14] Andrews, *People Called Shakers,* p. 233.

[15] Evans to Tolstoy, March 6, 1891, quoted in Morse, *Shakers and the World's People,* p. 235. A nineteenth-century American traveler, Andrew Dickson White, made a visit to Russia, where he met and talked with Tolstoy and later wrote: "He [Tolstoy] then went on to express an interest in the Shakers, and especially in Frederick Evans. He had evidently formed an idea of them very unlike the reality; in fact, the Shaker his imagination had developed was as different from a Lebanon Shaker as an eagle from a duck." Dickson, *Autobiography,* Walks and Talks with Tolstoi, March 1894. See *www.worldwideschool.org/library/books/hst/biography/AutobiographyofAndrewDicksonWhiteVolume2/chap5.html.*

[16] Bradford, Roderick. *D. M. Bennett: The Truth Seeker.* Amherst, NY: Prometheus Books, 2006, p. 120. Bennett, after leaving the Shakers in his youth, published a magazine called *The Truth Seeker,* a "free-thought" publication with a readership of over fifty thousand that included Mark Twain and Clarence Darrow. Bennett announced that there was no proof for the existence of God, scoffed at the divinity of the Bible, and advocated the abolition of religion. However, he maintained a high regard for the Shakers he had once fled, and visited them frequently throughout his life. "This is about the only Christian body that believes in liberty of thought and speech," he wrote (Bradford, *The Truth Seeker,* p. 132). The sixty-year-old editor, at the conclusion of a sensational trial, was sentenced to a year's hard labor for sending obscenity through the mail.

[17] New Lebanon Ministry to Canterbury Ministry, July 19, 1863. In the collection of the Shaker Museum and Library, Old Chatham, NY.

[18] Ibid.

[19] Ibid.

[20] Schlissel, *Conscience in America,* p. 122.

[21] Brock, Peter. *Pacifism in the United States From the Colonial Era to the First World War.* Princeton, NJ: Princeton University Press, 1968, p. 829.

Seasoned with Grace

Behold, I send you forth as sheep in the midst of wolves:
be ye therefore wise as serpents, and harmless as doves.

— Saying of Jesus to His apostles, Matthew 10:16[1]

A smoke-belching locomotive crawled into the Washington, DC, train station and came to a clanging, hissing halt. Two men, dressed alike in sober coats and broad-brimmed straw hats, descended from the train, mingling with the rest of the crowd on the platform. Elder Frederick Evans was accompanied by another New Lebanon Elder, Benjamin Gates.

The packed station was full of soldiers: men hobbling on crutches, men on litters, men with missing eyes, legs, or arms. Nurses, doctors, and anxious relatives hovered around the patients. Wagons delivered coffins to be loaded into departing trains, which would carry the embalmed bodies of soldiers back to their home states for burial.

The two Shakers emerged from the station into a crowded city that was the heart of the Union war machine. As well as being the seat of the federal government, Washington had become a major medical center, with many buildings turned into hospitals. The city was bustling from dawn to midnight.

Another visitor to Washington, a few months before, was a young author, Louisa May Alcott, who had volunteered to nurse the wounded. She described her arrival in the nation's capitol with awe. "Though I'd often been told that Washington was a spacious place, its visible magnitude quite took my breath away...The White House was lighted up, and carriages were rolling in and out of the great gate . . . Pennsylvania Avenue, with its bustle, lights, music, and military, made me feel as if I'd crossed the water and landed somewhere in Carnival time."[2]

Fresh from the sleepy town of Concord, Massachusetts, she was astonished at the racket in the streets. "Long trains of army wagons kept up a perpetual rumble from morning to night; ambulances rattled to and fro with busy surgeons, nurses taking an airing, or convalescents going in parties to be fitted to artificial limbs."[3]

Frederick Evans might have been reminded of the Shaker Sisters, modestly attired in chaste white caps, when he saw the passing ladies, whom Alcott described as "so extinguished in their three-story bonnets, with overhanging balconies of flowers, that their charms were obscured." The Elders, dressed in their drab coats and plain hats, were a distinct contrast to the gentlemen and officers, whom Alcott seemed to admire more than she did the ladies. "The men did the picturesque, and did it so well that Washington looked like a mammoth masquerade. Spanish hats, scarlet-lined riding-cloaks, swords and sashes, high boots and bright spurs . . . gallant riders of gaily caparisoned horses . . . prancing by."[4]

But Evans and Gates had no time for sight-seeing. They marched purposefully towards the White House. The Elders made their way along the crowded streets, dodging mule-drawn carts, galloping army couriers bearing urgent dispatches, tourists, columns of recruits. Ankle-deep mud mingled with horse and mule droppings, and "rowdy pigs pushed the passers by off the side walk."[5] Washington's humidity made the smell of the livestock stronger, mingled with odors of restaurants, laundries, and chamber pots from the many hospitals.

Brother Benjamin Gates already knew his way around Washington. In the fall of 1862, a Shaker named George Ingals had been drafted into the state militia. Gates went to Washington to try to get Ingals exempted, and the stubborn Elder left no stone unturned — he met with Secretary of War Edwin Stanton, Secretary of State

William Seward, and briefly, Lincoln himself. Gates succeeded in obtaining exemption papers for Ingals. In addition, "Br Benjamin also received instructions from government, that, if any more of the Shakers . . . were drafted, that, by forwarding their names and a certificate of their nonresistant principles, and conscientious scruples, to Washington, the reprieve papers should be furnished for them."[6]

This success must have seemed, at the time, to put an end to fears of conscription. However, in the way of governmental bureaucracies, these somewhat vague directions do not seem to have made their way down the chain of command, and when the federal draft notices went out in the summer of 1863, many bore the names of Shaker Brothers. So it was time for another assault on Washington.

The White House today, of course, is ringed with barricades, security checkpoints, and armed guards. An ordinary citizen has precious little chance of stopping by and paying an uninvited visit to the President of the United States. Lincoln's White House, however, was astonishingly casual. Visitors strolled in and out. Lincoln himself often trudged, completely unguarded, across the White House lawn and over to the nearby War Department, to hear how things were going at the front.

Even in those days, Lincoln was considered unusual for his accessibility. Noah Brooks, a friend and frequent visitor, wrote, "The multitude, washed or unwashed, always has free egress and ingress."[7] The stairs to the president's office were often packed with lines of people waiting to see him. All kinds of folk came: office-seekers, well-wishers, irate citizens with complaints about taxes, amateur strategists with advice on how to win the war — almost anyone could get in to see Abraham Lincoln.

Evans and Gates, like other visitors, entered the White House beneath an "immense portico, whose tall columns stand thickly," which led into "a small vestibule [that] opens into a wide hall, handsomely carpeted."[8] The Elders must have raised their eyebrows at the White House décor. "The ceiling is frescoed, . . . cupids, flowers and such sprawling about overhead in a very loose manner, the unbreeched urchins looking as though a suit of Uncle Sam's uniform would not come amiss this cold weather." Noah Brooks went on to describe the "lace curtains, heavy cords and tassels and damask drapery . . . gorgeous carpet . . . [and] heavy crimson satin window hangings," and noted with annoyance that visitors would often snip a souvenir out of the curtains.[9]

The president generally began his office hours in the morning. "It is very much of a lottery as to who shall get in first," wrote Brooks. "The gratified applicant . . . may have been cooling his heels outside for five minutes or five days, but is now ushered into a large square room."[10]

Lincoln's office was not the famous oval room we see in news clips today. He used a long, rectangular room in the East Wing, (now famous as the Lincoln Bedroom, although he never used it as such.) He worked at a battered writing desk, with pigeonholes stuffed full of letters. A large table in the middle of the room was generally piled high with maps and books. Over the fireplace was a portrait of Andrew Jackson. There was a comfortable horsehair sofa in the room, and Tad, Lincoln's young son, sometimes napped there while his father worked.

This untidy room was the hub of that busy war-time White House. Cabinet meetings were held around the big table. Here Lincoln read his mail, signed documents, dealt with officials, entertained guests, and had his hair and beard trimmed. From the window he could see the blunt rectangle of the half-finished Washington Monument, and in the distance the encampments of Union soldiers.

The Shaker Elders, entering the Chief Executive's inner sanctum, must have glanced curiously around the room. Frederick Evans, crusader for health, was extremely critical of the housekeeping arrangements that prevailed in the World; he despised carpeted rooms "with piles of dust beneath, never swept away, and of which I had to breathe," and referred to picture frames as "the receptacles of dust."[11] He may have cast a disapproving eye over the president's cluttered office. The Shakers' bare wooden floors and plain, peg-boarded rooms were a stark contrast to Lincoln's loudly patterned rug, heavy draperies, and vivid wallpaper.

"Well?" Lincoln would inquire of visitors, brows raised, spectacles low on his nose. "What can I do for you?"[12] He was blunt and informal, but many of the thousands who met him recorded that he was polite, warm, and attentive. "Few, if any, went away without being favorably impressed by his hearty Western greeting, and the frank sincerity of his manner and conversation," his secretary noted.[13]

Lincoln's great height, made more noticeable by his leanness, struck every observer. But journalist James Gilmore, who met Lincoln often, wrote that the president "was not — as very tall men often are — ungainly in either manner or attitude. As he leaned back in his chair, he had an air of unstudied ease, a kind of careless dignity." Many people remarked that Lincoln was ugly; Gilmore agreed that "he impressed me as a very homely man . . . but this was before I had seen him smile, or met the glance of his deep set, dark gray eye — the deepest, saddest, and yet kindliest eye I had ever seen in a human being."[14]

Lincoln did, indeed, have a very striking face. He is arguably the most recognizable figure in American history; we see his face, gazing solemnly into eternity, every time we spend a penny or a five-dollar bill. It is tantalizing to imagine what the stern face looked like in life, the lips parting in a smile, the eyes lit up with welcome, as he peered over the spectacles on his nose.

Most of the existing photographs of Lincoln are formal and solemn. Given the photographic technology of those days, snapshots were impossible — Lincoln had to hold completely still, often with the back of his head held in a metal immobilizing frame, for the camera to achieve an unblurred image. But a few pictures exist which show Lincoln wearing a slight smile — his son Tad was sometimes present at photo sessions, and the president was captured for posterity with an amused and loving light in his eyes as he watched his lively son's antics.

Photographs of both Frederick Evans and Henry Blinn, taken in their old age, show vigorous men who are younger-looking than was Lincoln in his early fifties. The Shaker life of manual work, sensible nutrition, and excellent medical care kept Shakers in good health generally, and they tended to have life-spans that were significantly longer than the national average.[15] Perhaps their faith in Divine Providence also helped to keep their faces unlined.

Lincoln's gaunt face (Figure 9) showed the burden of the years of war: the lost battles, the bitter criticism, the endless casualty lists. And another grief had recently carved new lines in his face; his beloved twelve-year-old son, Willie, had died the year before. Lincoln was a fond and indulgent parent who delighted in playing with his sons, and he was devastated by the child's death. For months afterwards he sometimes shut himself in a room to weep unobserved.

The Shakers put their case to the president. Lincoln generally did not rush his visitors, as Brooks observed with some exasperation. "He is not good at dispatching business, but lets every person use more time than he might if the interview were strictly limited to the real necessities of the case."[16] Abraham Lincoln likely heard the Shakers out with patient interest.

Evans, an articulate man well accustomed to interpreting the Shaker way to non-Believers, must have eloquently explained their deeply-felt commitment to non-violence. As he spoke, he may have remembered Mother Ann's famous admonition — odd advice from such an outspoken woman: "Let your words be few, and seasoned with grace."[17]

Evans urged the Shakers' long tradition of pacifism as a reason for exempting them from the draft. But he had another, more prosaic, argument up his sleeve.

He pointed out a fact that the War Office had apparently never considered: an appreciable number of the Brethren had served in the armed forces before they joined the Shakers. These veterans had never claimed any of their pensions, in accordance with the Shaker belief that war, and profiting from war, was wrong. Mother

Figure 9. This last photograph of Lincoln was taken by Alexander Gardner, April 10, 1865 — four days before Lincoln was assassinated by John Wilkes Booth. Use courtesy of The Granger Collection, New York, NY.

Ann had instructed Revolutionary War veterans who joined the Shakers that they should refuse any financial assistance from the government, saying that a pension was "the price of blood," and this had been the Shakers' practice ever since.[18]

If, however, the Shakers now laid claim to all these back benefits, the United States government might be legally obligated to pay them a considerable sum. With characteristic precision, the

Shakers had determined that the amount they were owed was exactly $1,032,873.77.[19]

This was rather a good deal of money in the days when an army private's salary was $13 a month. The North was struggling with financial hard times and war-induced inflation, and the president cannot have been anxious to engage in expensive and time-consuming litigation.

The Elders did not rely only on verbal persuasion; they had also written a formal document addressed to "His Excellency the President of the United States." It stated that the "United Society of Shakers . . . respectfully ask for exemption from service of such of the members of their society as may be drafted." They claimed that "non-resistance and non-participation in the affairs of earthly governments are primary and fundamental articles in the religious faith of the Shaker Societies."[20]

As Evans recalled, after the Shakers had presented their arguments, "President Lincoln leaned back in his chair and asked, 'Well, what am I to do?'"

Evans diplomatically replied, "'It is not for me to advise the President of the United States.'

"Looking at him appreciatively, President Lincoln exclaimed: 'You ought to be *made* to fight! We need regiments of just such men as you.'"[21]

We'll never know whether Abraham Lincoln was moved by practical considerations, or impressed by the Elders' eloquent arguments, high principles, and dignified bearing. Whatever the reason, the president agreed to accept the petition, thereby establishing the position of the Shakers as officially sanctioned conscientious objectors.

❧

"Tell them," Ann Lee had cried, a hundred years earlier, "that we are the people who turn the world upside down." Mother Ann and her earliest followers challenged the existing order of things, enduring whips, stones, and the World's mockery. The Elders' courteous visit to the White House was less dramatic, but it was effective. The Shakers' exemption from the draft, coming shortly after the first federal conscription act, was a precedent of deep significance.

The Shakers weren't alone in their fight. Quakers and clergymen of several denominations had also been agitating for exemption. They blazed a trail for all future conscientious objectors to follow, by persuading the United States government to acknowledge that there were citizens who believed that war was wrong, and, further, that citizens had a right to act on that belief.

In February, 1864, the United States Congress revised the Conscription Act. "That members of religious denominations, who shall by oath or affirmation declare that they are conscientiously opposed to the bearing of arms . . . shall when drafted into the military service, be considered non-combatants." They could be assigned to "duty in the hospitals, or to the care of freedmen."[22] This was the first national legislation dealing with conscientious objection.

In the years that followed, filled with war after devastating war, hundreds of thousands of conscientious objectors followed the Shakers' example; they fought, within the system, to obtain legal status. During World War I and World War II, thousands of men who regarded war as a sin served in the military as noncombatants, or did public service. During the Vietnam War, there were 170,000 officially recognized conscientious objectors.[23]

As Shakers had once challenged the World's definitions of God and family, now they helped to redefine its obligations of citizenship. The Shakers, once again, had shaken up the World.

Notes

[1] *Holy Bible.*

[2] Alcott, Louisa May. *Hospital Sketches*. Bedford, MA: Applewood Books, 1993, p. 23. Louisa May Alcott would later gain fame as a novelist for children, but her first best-seller was a vivid account of her nursing days, called *Hospital Sketches*. This short book was a moving portrayal of the soldiers' suffering, and an unvarnished account of the aftermath of glorious victories. Published while the war was still raging, it fascinated a nation hungry for news of their loved ones.

[3] Ibid., p. 71.

[4] Ibid., p. 72.

[5] Ibid., p. 74.

[6] Central Ministry Journal 1859–1874; October 28, 1862. In the collection of the Shaker Museum and Library, Old Chatham, NY.

[7] Brooks, *Lincoln Observed*, p. 80.

[8] Ibid.

[9] Ibid., p. 82.

[10] Ibid., p. 84.

[11] Sprigg, *By Shaker Hands*, p. 112

[12] Brooks, *Lincoln Observed*, p. 85.

[13] Nicolay, John G. *A Short Life of Abraham Lincoln*. New York, NY: The Century Company, 1902, p. 158.

[14] Gilmore, James R. *Personal Recollections of Abraham Lincoln and the Civil War*. Mechanicsburg, PA: Stackpole Books, 2007, p. 14.

[15] Andrews, *Work and Worship*, p. 74. One Shaker, "Mother Dolly" Saxton, "came to the Shakers on her fifth birthday," and celebrated "not only the beginning of her 106th year, but her hundredth anniversary as a Shakeress." *The Shaker Manifesto*, June 1881, vol. 11, no. 6, p. 134.

[16] Brooks, *Lincoln Observed*, p. 85.

[17] *Testimonies*, p. 257.

[18] White and Taylor, *Shakerism*, p. 178. Amos Buttrick, a Shaker Brother who was a veteran, accepted a pension after the Revolutionary War. But his conscience troubled him, and although the Shakers at the time were suffering "poverty and great privation" he returned the money to amazed officials in the Treasury Office, who gave him a receipt for "Eighty-two pound, seven shillings, and eight pence."

[19] Blinn, *Record*, p. 187. This figure, precise to the penny, is quoted in Henry Blinn's *Historical Record*, as an estimate made by the New Lebanon Shakers of the sum owed them by the United States government. White and Taylor's *Shakerism, Its Meaning and Message* quotes the document presented to Lincoln as stating that the government owed the Shakers $600,000, and that "the societies in Kentucky, not yet heard from, would materially augment this amount." White and Taylor, *Shakerism*, p. 183.

[20] White and Taylor, *Shakerism*, p. 182.

[21] Ibid.

[22] Schlissel, *Conscience in America*, p. 98.

[23] Tollefson, James W. *The Strength Not to Fight: Conscientious Objectors of the Vietnam War*. Washington, DC: Brassey's, Inc., 2000, p. 6.

Mr. Lincoln's Chair

Nov. 7 1863
Anthony Colby, Provost Marshal
2nd N.H. District

Henry C. Blinn

Furloughed until called for.[1]

Henry Blinn must have felt a surge of jubilant relief when he received this terse telegram. In four brief words, it put to rest his worst nightmare.

Perhaps he felt a sense of unease at the ominous phrase "until called for." However, the call never came. Pending the passing of amendments to the Conscription Act which would provide for conscientious objectors, baffled officials simply furloughed them indefinitely.

During the late summer and fall of 1863, the details of the exemption process dragged on, however, and it took yet another embassy to Edwin Stanton, Secretary of War, to finalize matters. A strongly-worded petition was dispatched from South Union Village Elders, addressed "To the Honorable Abraham Lincoln," and greeting him as "Kind Friend." South Union, Kentucky, was right in the thick of things during the war, as the Elders acidly pointed out. "Your armies have visited us, from a small squad to five to six thousand at a time. Our barns were cheerfully relieved of their contents, our fences turned into campfires…but gratuitously have we furnished food for thousands of your men." They implored Lincoln, in forthright language, to exempt Shakers from military service, as had the passing Confederate armies, arguing that if the Shaker principle of pacifism was "respected by the Confederate government can it be ignored by the Federal? . . . We ask for simple justice, nothing more."

The Elders had faith in Lincoln's judgment, and like so many, turned directly to the president for redress. "We look upon you, not only as the friend of humanity and the rights of man, but as the chosen instrument of God, in this time of the nation's peril."[2]

Abraham Lincoln did not fail the Shakers. The Brethren were left in peace for the remainder of the war.

The Shakers were deeply grateful for this consideration, and viewed the president as their benefactor. A gift, they felt, would be a tangible mark of their esteem. So the Shaker craftsmen set to work, to build a chair for Abraham Lincoln.

Take a look, sometime, on e-Bay, and check out what Shaker chairs are going for these days. Henry Blinn's jaw would drop. Collectors pay fabulous prices for the humblest footstool, as long as it is authentic Shaker handiwork. An empty Shaker flour sack once sold for hundreds of dollars. Ten thousand dollars is not a bad price for a cabinet or table. In 1990, a single piece of Shaker furniture, a simple work counter made of pine, was purchased by Oprah Winfrey for $220,000.[3] Furniture designers from Japan to Scandinavia have imitated Shaker designs, but the prices for the real thing keep skyrocketing.

Why are these unadorned objects, sneered at as "grim" in their own time, so valuable now? It's not only the clean, uncluttered lines, the beauty of the polished wood. It's the perfection in every smallest detail.

"The peculiar grace of a Shaker chair," wrote Thomas Merton, a twentieth-century monk and anti-Vietnam war activist, "is due to the fact that it was made by someone capable of believing that an angel might come and sit on it."[4] The Shakers' goal was to recreate a flawless heaven here on earth. Striving for perfection in one's work, no matter how humble the task, was an outward sign of inner striving for spiritual perfection. The best Shaker craftsmen and women measured every inch with precision, and rejected any piece that had a microscopic flaw.

The desks, baskets, and oval boxes they crafted are not only pleasing to the eye, but useful as well; they perfectly fulfill their function — the drawers don't stick, the legs don't wobble, the lids still fit snugly, even after decades of damp New England weather. "Trifles make perfection," went the Shaker maxim, "but perfection itself is no trifle."[5]

These high standards made Shaker commercial products famous for their quality. It may seem strange for such a devoutly religious group to be astute and successful businesspeople, but the Shakers, in their quest to ensure economic security for their communities, had early learned that one way to get the cash they needed was to sell their crafts and produce. Their genius for entrepreneurship was oddly enhanced by their religious zeal.

"It isn't loud praying that counts with the Lord so much as giving four quarts for every gallon, sixteen ounces for a pound, and thirty-six inches to the yard," an article in the Shakers' monthly publication, *The Shaker Manifesto,* stated firmly.[6] In an era before the US Food and Drug Administration inspected products to be sure they were fit for consumers to purchase, there was no way to be sure you were getting what you paid for. Unless the word "Shaker" was on the label. That was a guarantee of excellence. If you bought flour from a Shaker dealer, you could be sure that the barrel wasn't half filled with sawdust. Shaker butter was pure and creamy, not rancid, moldy, or eked out with axle grease. Shaker applesauce was sweet and fresh. Shaker garden seeds produced healthy, thriving plants.

Purchasing medicine was a hazardous occupation in the nineteenth century, and many an unfortunate patient died of the cure rather than the disease. Sellers of patent medicines made wildly outlandish claims, offering to cure every ailment from the common cold to old age. Many infallible nostrums were nothing but cheap alcohol or turpentine; others contained poisonous dyes, opium, or chloroform. Distrust of such quack medicines grew; one manufacturer went so far as to offer "five hundred dollars life insurance in case of death if you use this medicine."[7]

But if you bought Shaker products, you knew what you were getting. Shaker medicines contained the healing herbs and other ingredients they advertised; nothing more, nothing less.

The Shakers became a byword for integrity, and they found that it paid. Over time the Shakers developed scores of products. Henry Blinn wrote that at Canterbury Brothers and Sisters were "engaged in the manufacture of wrought and cut nails, brass clocks, candlesticks, skimmers and ladles, sieves, hats, tanning and currying of leather, shoemaking . . . wagons, wooden shovels . . . whips, hoes, scythes, tobacco boxes and the raising of garden seeds."[8] Their herbal medicine industry was the biggest in the nation. Not unlike China today, they had a large labor force and low overhead, combined with an aggressive marketing strategy. Shaker businesses brought in sums that today would be in the millions.[9]

"We have spared no expense or labor in our endeavors to produce an article that cannot be surpassed in any respect . . . which combines all of the advantages of durability, simplicity and lightness."[10]

So ran the announcement of Shaker chairs for sale in a widely-circulated catalog. By the latter half of the nineteenth century, chair-making was big business for some Shaker villages, notably New Lebanon, home of Frederick Evans. By the 1870s, they were even publishing an illustrated catalog, listing chairs sized 0 (for children) to size 7 (extra large.) Like most folk of those times, Shakers weren't restrained by any false modesty in their advertising. They boasted of "the care we take in our thorough selection of materials which are put into the chairs, and the excellent workmanship which is applied to their construction."[11]

But, unlike most advertisers, the Shakers claimed no more than the truth. The stark design is deceptive; if you try out a Shaker chair you might agree with Abraham Lincoln in finding it very comfortable. And the slim-legged chairs were not only durable but astonishingly light. As the catalog pointed out, "Our largest chairs do not weigh over ten pounds, and the smallest weigh less than five pounds." But they were solidly well-built in spite of their slight weight, and the description concluded reassuringly, "The largest person can feel safe in sitting down in them without fear of going through them."[12]

The Shakers had started selling chairs as early as 1789. They developed many variations on the basic pattern, especially in the chairs they made for their own use. Different tasks required different types of chairs. But whether the chair was a low-seated one for sorting apples or a high-legged one for ironing, the purpose was the same — to enable the worker to perform his or her daily labor with efficiency and in comfort. As usual, Shaker craftsmen put their ingenuity to work; they designed sewing chairs with built-in drawers, and students' seats with attached writing surfaces. They made wheeled chairs for the infirm, potty chairs for the very young and the very old, and a reclining chair for Henry Blinn's dentist shop. Trustees doing clerical work in busy offices used wheeled chairs with seats that turned from side to side, called "revolvers."

The peak of the chair-makers' art, however, was the rocking chair. Rockers were first made in the early 1700s, and folklore credits Benjamin Franklin as the inventor.[13] The rocking chair seems to be an American creation, perhaps befitting a country that formally included "the pursuit of happiness" in its national goals. The rocking chair had but one purpose — to give rest. Originally the Shakers used them only for the elderly, but by 1840 rocking chairs were standard in almost every retiring room, leading Elder Philemon Stewart to inquire sharply "How comes it about that there are so many rocking chairs used? Is the rising generation going to be able to keep the way of God, by seeking after ease?"[14]

We don't know what kind of chair the Shakers made for Lincoln. The chair itself has long since vanished into some forgotten attic of history. But it was quite probably a rocking chair, the most deluxe and expensive item in their catalog. It was well-known that Lincoln enjoyed a comfortable rocker; the owners of Ford's Theatre provided a special rocking chair for the president's use when he came to see a play. A "Big Arm Chair with rockers, cushioned," would sell, in those days, for about twelve dollars.[15]

∽

"Went into the east woods and hunted up a maple tree for chair backs. Thomas cut it down and we trimmed it out and sawed up the logs and got home to dinner."[16]

Brother Freegift Wells was a Shaker craftsman who created many beautiful pieces of furniture, often assisted by his young apprentice Thomas Almond. His journals give a detailed look at the process of crafting a Shaker chair.[17]

It's difficult for us, in the plastic age of the twenty-first century, to realize how people of earlier times depended on wood. "From cradle of wood to coffin of wood," writes historian Eric Sloane, "the life of man was encircled by it."[18] In past times, craftsmen knew trees as do few woodworkers today. A carpenter might walk through a forest, carefully choosing the trees to fell for a special project he had in mind.

Some individual trees were friends of long standing. A sewing desk made by Henry Blinn has an inscription on the bottom of a drawer: "These two Sewing desks were made from Mother Hannah's Butternut trees, grown South of Ministries Shop. Were cared for by her when saplings."[19]

Most carpenters of those days could identify a tree at a glance. Even in winter when the leaves were gone, the silvery gleam of maple bark was completely different from the corrugated trunk of an oak or the curving strips of shagbark hickory. From long experience, a craftsman would know the best use for each species — hard maple for chairs and tables, supple black ash for baskets, tough hickory for tool handles, durable black locust for fence posts that would last for decades.

After the tree was cut, the trunk was sawed into lengths along the grain. The wood was not kiln-dried, as is usual today; too-rapid drying seems to "kill the wood" and make it brittle.[20] The boards were stored in the attic to season slowly; a good craftsman allowed two years of seasoning for every inch of thickness.

In the eighteenth century, boards of over two feet in width were not uncommon, and an entire knot-free door or tabletop might be made from of a single piece of wood cut from a mammoth tree. A hundred years later, few virgin stands of forest remained; woodlots had been harvested too often, and a Shaker carpenter might have to walk a long way to "hunt up" trees of the proper size for his work.

The Shakers disdained fashionable imported woods like mahogany and teak. They used lumber that grew locally; the pale golden wood of the hard maple, also called sugar maple, was one of their favorites for furniture. One chair might have several types of woods — sturdy maple for the legs, birch or butternut for the back slats or arms.

Chair-making sounds like a soothing, tranquil job, but a Shaker carpentry shop was not an old-fashioned place with white-bearded craftsmen slowly whittling out chair legs by hand. Shakers used state-of-the-art water wheels and turbines to power saws, lathes, and drills. Some workshops had a host of power tools all noisily cutting and whirling and whirring simultaneously. The technology-hungry Shakers had early put water to many ingenious uses, from pressing apples for cider to cutting blocks of stone. Brothers began digging ponds and running underground pipes at some villages in the 1700s. One brook might turn half a dozen different millstones and water-wheels; neighbors who lived near the Canterbury Shakers joked that by the time the Shakers were done with a brook, they had used the water so many times that they had worn it out.

The unknown carpenter who crafted Lincoln's chair doubtless used power tools to shape the legs, rungs, and back posts. After using a buzz-saw to cut each piece to the proper size, the rough wood had to be carefully centered on a lathe, a kind of potter's wheel that spun the wood so that it could be shaped into a cylinder. Once the lathe was set up and working smoothly, an expert could turn out a beautifully-shaped chair leg in less than a minute.

In order to make a comfortable chair, the back had to be curved. The hard back slats were heated in a steam box so that the damp wood would bend without breaking. Slats, as well as the rockers for rocking chairs, were carefully bent on a clamping jig and held in place with C-clamps.[21] The wood dried slowly, keeping the shape of the graceful curve. Then the chair was assembled, slats and rungs securely fastened to the tall back posts, the side rungs added to complete the whole.

Choice pieces of Shaker-made furniture or tools were sometimes designed to fit the person who was to use them. The craftsmen who worked on Mr. Lincoln's chair surely took into account the president's height. Even those who had never met Lincoln in person would be well aware of the fact that he had a long back and unusually long legs (Figure 10), which were often lampooned in newspaper caricatures.

The precise Shakers kept exact recipes for stains and varnishes. Some finishes revealed the natural beauty of the wood, but most of their customers, and the Shakers themselves, seemed to prefer either a very dark finish, in ebony or mahogany tones, or startlingly bright colors. Henry Blinn, who visited the big New Lebanon chairworks, wrote that the chairs were "stained in a hot log wood dye which forces the color into the wood. When varnished they are bright red," probably a bit too bright for our modern eyes.[22]

So far the task had been strictly men's work, but now the women took over. To create chair seats, Sisters hand-wove long ribbons of brightly-dyed wool.[23] By this time the Shakers, like people in the World, had mostly abandoned the earlier plant dyes, and were using chemical dyes to produce intense hues like orange, scarlet,

Figure 10. Allan Pinkerton, Lincoln, and Major General John A. McClernand at Antietam, Maryland, 3 October 1862. Lincoln's long legs, great height, and trademark stove-pipe hat made him conspicuous wherever he went. Photograph by Alexander Gardner; use courtesy of The Granger Collection, New York, NY.

pomegranate, peacock blue, olive, and gold — "a great variety of the prettiest colors which can be produced," as the catalog cheerfully put it.[24] Some of the long ribbons of wool were solid colors, some were intricately patterned "mini-tapestries," a hundred feet long and an inch wide.[25]

The Sisters then wove these tapes over the seat frame, using a long, flat needle. They designed simple checkerboards of contrasting colors, or fancy herringbone patterns. Layers of padding in between the tapes made for a comfortable, sturdy seat. For the president, they may have added a luxury they seldom used themselves: thick plush cushions for the seat and back.

The result of this painstaking process was a chair of simple beauty. But Shaker philosophy was profoundly mistrustful of the beautiful. Millennial Laws warned that Shakers should "manufacture no object [that will] . . . feed the pride and vanity of man" or was "superfluous."[26] Shakers cultivated fields of flowers that were dazzling in their full bloom — but the flowers were to be considered as crops, harvested for the medicinal herb business, the seed trade, or to make the Shaker's famous rosewater, used for flavoring sweets. Wearing a rose in one's buttonhole, or decorating the Meeting House with vases of flowers, was not permitted.[27]

The Shaker craftspeople sought ideal form to fulfill each necessary function. Ironically, they created great beauty. Many years passed, however, before those who lived in the World could see it. Not until the 1920s did a few visionary antique collectors begin knocking on the doors of Shaker Dwelling Houses, offering to buy old chairs and tables. Now people around the world are moved by the simple elegance of Shaker designs.

꙾

Mr. Lincoln's chair, finished at last, was sent to the White House. No individual, as far as we know, was credited with its manufacture, and that was also according to doctrine. The 1845 Millennial Laws decreed that no work of the hands was to be signed — although this was a rule that was frequently neglected. Even Elders like Henry Blinn signed their work sometimes. One rebellious furniture maker, Brother Orren Haskins, signed some of his pieces in letters three inches high.[28] But most Shakers crafted their masterpieces anonymously. Even in death, Shakers were often buried under tombstones marked only with initials.

The Shaker chair arrived at the White House, amid the usual flood of letters and other gifts. Many of the givers, of course, had a hidden agenda. So many people wanted something from the harassed president: jobs, recommendations, pardons, autographs, favors. One entrepreneur sent a supply of "Dr. E. Cooper's Universal Magnetic Balm," recommended for everything from cramps to Cholera Morbus, and confidently requested an endorsement.[29]

The courteous Lincoln sent a thank-you note to the Shakers, personally signed.

> *Washington, August 8th, 1864*
> *My good friends,*
>
> *I wish to express to you my cordial thanks for the very comfortable chair you sent me some time since, and to tell you how gratefully I appreciate the kindness which prompted the present.*
>
> *And I must beg that you will pardon the length of time that, through an oversight in my office, has elapsed without an acknowledgment of your kindness.*
>
> *I am very truly*
> *Your friend and obt servt.*
> *A. Lincoln[30]*

A close observer once described Abraham Lincoln as having a manner "quiet, chaste, and dignified . . . simple, direct, and almost religious . . . an indefinable something." Those perceptive words might well serve as a description of a Shaker chair.[31]

At any rate, the Brothers and Sisters had done their work well; perhaps the overworked, war-weary president could stretch out his long legs and take some rest in his "very comfortable chair."

Notes

[1] Blinn, *Record,* vol. 1, p. 299.

[2] White and Taylor, *Shakerism,* p. 197.

[3] Stein, *Shaker Experience,* p. 406.

[4] Andrews, Edward Deming, and Faith Andrews. *Religion in Wood: A Book of Shaker Furniture.* Bloomington, IN: Indiana University Press, 1982, p. xiii.

[5] *The Manifesto,* March 1899, vol. 29, no. 3, p. 33.

[6] *The Shaker Manifesto,* June 1881, vol. 11, no. 6, p. 134.

[7] Bowen, Ezra, editor. *This Fabulous Century.* Morristown, NJ: Time/Life Books, Silver Burdett Co., 1970, p. 217.

[8] Blinn, *Record,* vol. 1, p. 246.

[9] Miller, Amy Bess. *Shaker Medicinal Herbs: A Compendium of History, Lore, and Uses.* New York, NY: N. Potter, Inc., 1976, p. 3. One of the Shakers' many inventions that we still use today is the paper seed packet. Until the mid-nineteenth century, merchants only sold seeds for cash crops like oats or corn, in bulk. Shakers devised the idea of putting flower and vegetable seeds in convenient packets for family gardens. The seed packets were widely marketed, sometimes displayed on countertops in attractive boxes which were confidently labeled *Shakers' Choice Vegetable Seeds Always Produce Splendid Vegetables.*

[10] From the Shakers' 1874 chair catalog, in Muller, Charles R., and Timothy D. Rieman. *The Shaker Chair.* Atglen, PA: Schiffer Publishing, Ltd., 2003, p. 170.

[11] Ibid.

[12] Ibid.

[13] Benjamin Franklin, while probably not the sole inventor of the rocking chair, owned one of the first in America. With Shaker-like ingenuity, he also designed a rocker-powered fan.

[14] Muller and Rieman, *Shaker Chair,* p. 145.

[15] Diary of James Prescott, North Union, October 5, 1860, in Muller and Rieman, *Shaker Chair,* p. 152.

[16] Muller and Rieman, *Shaker Chair,* p. 14.

[17] Grant, Jerry V., and Douglas R. Allen. *Shaker Furniture Makers.* Hanover, NH: University Press of New England, 1989, pp. 22–33.

[18] Sloane, Eric. *A Reverence for Wood.* New York, NY: Funk and Wagnalls, Inc., 1965, p. 72.

[19] Grant and Allen, *Shaker Furniture Makers,* p. 151.

[20] Moser, Thomas. *How to Build Shaker Furniture.* New York, NY: Sterling Publishing Co., Inc., 1977, p. 17.

[21] Ibid., p. 143.

[22] Muller and Rieman, *Shaker Chair,* p. 200.

[23] In the early 1800s, many Shaker chairs were seated with rushes or splints, but by the 1860s Shakers were beginning to use the woolen tapes that were standard by the 1870s. We don't know what seating was used for Lincoln's chair, but it seems likely that the Shakers used their finest woven wool tapes.

[24] Muller and Rieman, *Shaker Chair,* p. 170.

[25] Rieman, Timothy D. *Shaker Furniture: A Craftsman's Journal.* Atglen, PA: Schiffer Publishing, 2006, p. 116.

[26] Sprigg, *Shaker Hands,* p. 84.

[27] Burns, *Shaker Cities,* p. 79.

[28] Rieman, *Furniture,* p. 93.

[29] Holzer, *Dear Mr. Lincoln,* p. 202.

[30] Abraham Lincoln to New Lebanon Shakers, August 8, 1864. In the collection of the Shaker Museum and Library, Old Chatham, NY.

[31] Wilson, Rufus Rockwell. *Intimate Memories of Lincoln.* Elmira, NY: The Primavera Press, 1945, p. 179.

The Great Crime

> *No more shall war, with direful curse*
> *Stain earth with human gore.*
> *Contending armies fight for right,*
> *The reign of sin is o'er.*
>
> — Frederick Evans[1]

As the winds and rain of March, 1865, began to thaw the New Hampshire winter, life was beginning to settle back to normal at Canterbury. The war was plainly all but over. The stubborn Confederates were holding on by their fingernails, but they were desperately short of men and supplies; the fighting couldn't last much longer. And the terrible yoke of slavery was being lifted from the nation. Henry Blinn recorded with deep thanksgiving that "Human beings are no longer held in chains of slavery and bought and sold like cattle . . . The Emancipation Proclamation, that message from God, has made the United States a free country."[2]

The New Lebanon Elders, however, were concerned that spring about their benefactor, President Lincoln. Perhaps Frederick Evans, a man keenly attuned to the spiritual, had divined some of Lincoln's inner turmoil, or perhaps he simply read the weariness in the president's lined face. But the Shakers were worried about one whom they considered a friend, and thought that Lincoln was in dire need of rest.

They were right. Lincoln was, indeed, not in good health. After the ceremonies of his second Inauguration, on March 4, 1865, the president was so exhausted that he spent several days in bed. He had lost a good deal of weight, and his long figure was becoming cadaverous; his face was gaunt, the cheekbones protruding, the lines around his eyes carved deeper than ever.

One evening, a few days after the Inauguration, he attended a theater, where he encountered one Colonel James Wilson, who inquired if Lincoln was enjoying the entertainment. The president answered wearily, "I have not come for the play, but for the rest. I am being hounded to death by office-seekers, who pursue me early and late, and it is simply to get two or three hours relief that I am here."[3]

The Shakers, deeply concerned about their friend, thought they had a cure for his fatigue. On March 19, 1865, the New Lebanon Elders sent a letter to Abraham Lincoln, whom they addressed as their "Esteemed friend." They invited the president to take a vacation.

In the short letter, the Elders explained that he would benefit from a visit to "our quiet home in Mt. Lebanon, as a place of rest for body and mind." They suggested that he come incognito, leaving behind "the President in Washington to be worshipped and worried." The Elders had seen first-hand how Lincoln was besieged with demands and criticism. "We will ask for no favors, and you shall hear no complaints; nor any petitions except to God for the restoration of your health and that you may be strengthened to accomplish your allotted tasks in the order of Divine Providence." Benjamin Gates and Frederick Evans both signed the letter.[4]

And, worried that Lincoln would not admit the urgent need for the restoration of his health, they included a note to secretaries Stanton and Seward. "Enclosed is a letter to the Man Abraham Lincoln. If you will send and entrust him to us, we will nurse him up with the 'milk of human kindness' administered by Common Sense. He shall receive just such treatment as we accord to each other, in similar cases; where the action of the brain has been too much in excess of that of the muscles."

The Elders promised to provide the president with "Plain simple food and rest: and attendants with cheerful faces." They closed by stating that the invitation was "in gratitude for favors received and in behalf of the Shaker Order."[5]

∾

As far as is known, no reply was made to these letters. Lincoln received up to five hundred letters a day, and obviously could not read all of them. He originally had only one official secretary, later augmented by two more. These harassed and hard-working individuals gave most letters short shrift: "After a proper examination almost all business letters were promptly referred to the special office, war, navy, &c., to which their matter related," wrote William O. Stoddard, one of the overworked secretaries. "Another large class — indeed, the largest, as a general thing — went into my willow waste-basket . . . three or four in a hundred . . . were laid on the President's desk."[6]

President Lincoln, of course, received innumerable invitations — to balls, charity fund-raisers, dinners, parades. Aware of his heavy responsibilities as a war-time leader, he accepted almost none of these enticing offers. One of the rare exceptions was an invitation to make "a few appropriate remarks" at the dedication of the cemetery at Gettysburg, where he gave the brief speech always thereafter known as the Gettysburg Address.[7] If Lincoln received the Shakers' invitation, he did not take advantage of it.

Others, however, agreed with the Shakers that a change of scene would benefit the weary president. Lincoln received another invitation, written the day after the one the Shakers sent in vain. It came in the form of a telegram in cipher from General Grant. "Can you not visit City Point [army headquarters] for a day or two? I would like very much to see you and I think the rest would do you good."[8] So Lincoln left Washington in late March, but not for New Lebanon; he visited Army headquarters and then followed closely behind Grant's troops as they moved through Virginia in pursuit of Lee's ragged, limping army.

∾

On April 1, a bitter fight at a crucial crossroads called Five Forks ended in a Union victory. The desperate Confederates were forced back, their supply lines cut. General Lee warned Jefferson Davis to evacuate Richmond, the Confederate capital. The retreating army fired warehouses and strategic buildings before they left, and looters also set fires. Half of the business district burned to the ground, leaving much of Richmond a blackened ruin. The smoke-stained remnants of brick walls and chimneys towered precariously over deserted streets, when, on April 4, Abraham Lincoln set out to visit the devastated city.

The Confederates had mined and obstructed the James River near Richmond, so that Lincoln had to leave his large vessel and take to a small barge, rowed by a handful of sailors. Smoke was still rising from the wreckage when the president disembarked inconspicuously, his arrival at first unnoticed. But soon his distinctive long-tailed coat and stove-pipe hat attracted attention, and he was recognized. Eager crowds of black citizens surrounded him, cheering wildly. One story recounts that an old man fell to his knees, shouting, "Bless the Lord, Father Abraham's come!"

"Don't kneel to me," Lincoln replied. "That is not right. You must kneel to God only, and thank him for the liberty you will hereafter enjoy."[9] Oddly enough, the president was (doubtless unconsciously) echoing the words of Mother Ann, who told a young convert, "Don't kneel to me...but kneel to God; for I am but your fellow servant."[10]

The president, holding his twelve-year-old son Tad by the hand, walked quietly through the streets of the enemy capital. Guarded at first only by the sailors from the barge, he eventually encountered a squad of Union soldiers, who escorted him to the Confederate White House. Lincoln toured the recently abandoned building, resting for a time in Jefferson Davis's study. Later, he stopped at the Virginia Statehouse, where the Confederate Congress had met, and which showed signs of hasty departure; chairs and tables were overturned, and now-worthless Confederate bonds were drifted on the floor.

News of his surprise visit spread. Crowds of cheering or curious people flocked to see him. His staff begged him to take more care of his personal safety in a place where so many hated him, but he had always been dismissive of death threats. Lincoln replied, "I cannot bring myself to believe that any human being lives who would do me any harm."[II]

He left Richmond in the afternoon, and soon returned to Washington to wait impatiently for news — which was not long in coming. On the morning of April 10, a five-hundred-gun salute thundered over the city to announce the joyful tidings of Lee's surrender the day before. Throngs of shouting, singing people surrounded the White House, eager to get a glimpse of Lincoln; they cheered wildly for the irrepressible Tad, who popped up at a window waving a Confederate flag. Finally Lincoln appeared. He did not give a formal speech, but asked the band to play "Dixie," which he declared was one of his favorite songs.

The war was virtually over, and Lincoln's spirits soared. On April 14, four weeks after the Shakers' invitation, he was still fatigued but in a celebratory mood. He did not go to New Lebanon for the rest he so badly needed; he and Mrs. Lincoln decided to attend a performance of the hit comedy "Our American Cousin" at Ford's Theatre.

A New Lebanon Sister, Cecelia De Vere, had a strange dream on an April night of that eventful year of 1865. Sister Cecelia, who had emigrated from Ireland as a child in the 1840s, sometimes sang aloud in her sleep, and other Sisters recorded her songs and visions. It was "the night after the announcement of the taking of Richmond," when the young Irish Sister had the strangest dream of all.

"I dreamed that I was at a theatre," Sister Cecelia remembered. "A splendid place, remarkable for its drapery of flags and brilliant lighting . . . A man seemed to walk on the air out of one of the boxes; a flag flew after him, but he trampled on the end of it and disappeared. In a moment there was a wild commotion, such that the whole assembly swayed like people in anguish." The weird scene was accompanied by ominous words. "Distinctly through the tumult that prevailed was whispered, 'For the great crime they are to be executed before the people, when the hour strikes.'"

The images she had envisioned while asleep filled her with forboding. "The dream . . . so burdened me that when it was related it made a deep impression on all who heard it. Eleven days after, the news of the assassination reached Mount Lebanon."[12]

Sister Cecelia's vivid account of her dream well describes the shocked and bewildered crowd in the flag-draped Ford's Theatre, on the night of April 14, 1865 (Figure 11). Lincoln had been sitting in a comfortable rocker especially provided by the theater, holding hands with his wife as he watched the play, when John Wilkes Booth walked silently up behind him. After firing the fatal shot, Booth made a leap from the presidential box to the stage, but in his haste he caught his heel in some patriotic drapery; as he fell, the shreds of a flag trailed from his spur. Then, as Sister Cecelia described, he disappeared from the wild commotion in the theater. Booth managed to escape from Washington, but Federal troops tracked him down. The assassin was shot and killed, and four of his accomplices were later hanged for Lincoln's murder.

∽

The Shakers, like the rest of the nation, were appalled by "the great crime." No Christian spirit of forgiveness filled the heart of the anonymous Shaker who wrote "The evil genius of this dark fiendish rebellion has given to the wide world an exhibition of the venom that rankled in the heart of the nation in the diabolical assassination of its chief magistrate."[13]

A service of mourning was held "in every family of Believers . . . on the occasion of President Lincoln's funeral." According to Eldress Anna White, the same hymn was used at all the services, "although without any previous arrangement or understanding."[14] This

Figure 11. The assassination of President Abraham Lincoln by John Wilkes Booth at Ford's Theatre, Washington, D.C., April 14, 1865. This contemporary color engraving echoes Sister Cecelia De Vere's account of her dream of a "great crime" in a theater. Use courtesy of The Granger Collection, New York, NY.

lament, later titled "Supplication in a Nation's Calamity," had first been heard in the winter of 1862, when it was sung by Sister Cecelia three times over in her sleep.[15] A verse shows the Shakers' deep concern with slavery:

> *Lord, may the bands of the captive be broken,*
> *O! may this struggle bring true liberty,*
> *Teach man that love is a heaven born token*
> *And that the truth alone can make him free.*[16]

Abraham Lincoln long held a special place in the hearts of many Shakers. Lincoln's birthday was celebrated as a holiday for years afterwards. The meeting with the beloved president was well remembered; it was a favorite tale that Elder Frederick Evans "used often to relate."[17]

❦

In spite of the death of the commander-in-chief, the long, bitter war was finally dwindling to its end. Many, on both sides, greeted peace with profound relief.

Peace was no less welcome to the Shakers. Some villages had been reduced to conditions of abject poverty, but with the end of hostilities, the enormous wartime taxes would lessen, and goods and livestock would no longer be confiscated or stolen. Commerce could resume in the reunified nation. And no more would Shaker Brothers have the danger of conscription hanging over their heads.

It must have seemed a bright prospect from the high Canterbury hilltop, as Henry Blinn looked out over the fields covered with the first green shoots of spring. Finally, the bad times were over, and things could get back to normal. Surely, peace and prosperity for the Shakers were just over the horizon.

Notes

[1] White and Taylor, *Shakerism*, p. 343.

[2] Blinn, *Memoriam*, p. 9. Technically, the Emancipation Proclamation only freed slaves in states or regions of states that were in rebellion, but Henry's enthusiasm was shared by many Abolitionists. The Thirteenth Amendment to the Constitution was ratified in December, 1865, finally ending slavery nationwide.

[3] Donald, *Lincoln*, p. 570.

[4] New Lebanon Elders to Abraham Lincoln, March 19, 1865. In the collection of the Shaker Museum and Library, Old Chatham, NY.

[5] New Lebanon Elders to Stanton and Seward, March 19, 1865. In the collection of the Shaker Museum and Library, Old Chatham, NY.

[6] Holzer, Harold, editor. *The Lincoln Mailbag: America Writes to the President, 1861–1865*. Carbondale, IL: Southern Illinois University Press, 1998, Introduction, p. *xxx*.

[7] David Wills to Abraham Lincoln, November 2, 1863, quoted in Holzer, *Dear Mr. Lincoln*, p. 287.

[8] Ulysses S. Grant to Abraham Lincoln, March 20, 1865, quoted in Holzer, *Dear Mr. Lincoln*, p. 300.

[9] Donald, *Lincoln*, p. 576.

[10] *Testimonies*, p. 329.

[11] Donald, *Lincoln*, p. 577.

[12] White and Taylor, *Shakerism*, p. 366.

[13] Clark, *Pleasant Hill in the Civil War*, p. 63.

[14] White and Taylor, *Shakerism*, p. 345.

[15] Patterson, *Shaker Spiritual*, p. 435. Darryl Thompson reports the use of another title: "A Prayer for the Captive."

[16] Patterson, *Shaker Spiritual*, p. 436.

[17] White and Taylor, *Shakerism*, p. 181.

The Valley of
Love and Delight

'Tis the gift to be simple,
  'Tis the gift to be free;
'Tis the gift to come down where we ought to be;
  And when we find ourselves in the place just right,
'Twill be in the valley of love and delight.

— "Simple Gifts," 1848[1]

As a boy in Providence, Rhode Island, Henry Blinn must have walked along the shore and played on the beach. He doubtless knew the feeling of standing ankle-deep in the surf to feel a retreating wave wash the sand from underfoot. For him, the Shakers' world was an island of peace, love, and creativity . . . but it was inexorably crumbling away, a grain at a time. The slow decline could no more be reversed than the turn of the tide.

Shaker enrollment peaked in the 1830s, when there were perhaps as many as 6,000 members. Then, imperceptibly at first, their numbers began to fall off.

Even in the Shakers' earliest days, there had been a steady stream of apostasies, especially among young men, causing much grief to the Elders.[2] One by one, or two by two, more Brothers and Sisters began to slip away — perhaps a couple would run off to get married (or not); a young man might be lured by the dream of making a fortune in the gold fields, out West; a skilled craftsman, tired of anonymity, might choose to open his own business in the World. Elderly Shakers passed away in the natural course of time, but fewer youngsters joined to replace them. It's hard to say when Henry might have felt the first thread of unease, as he noticed the vacant retiring rooms and the empty seats in the dining hall.

The wild spirituality of "Mother Ann's Work" had seemed a renewal of the original fervor of the Shakers; Believers hoped this would bring converts "flocking like doves" as in the old days. But, ultimately, it had the opposite effect. Some of the moderate, better-educated Shakers became skeptical when informed that they were being addressed by divine spirits such as "Holy Mother Wisdom," or "Laughing John," an African-American spirit who spread the "gift" of hysterical laughter through the congregation. More and more Shakers drifted away. As the Civil War ended, the exodus of Shakers accelerated at frightening speed.

There was no single explanation for this. Often, critics of the Shakers point gleefully to celibacy as the cause of the decline in enrollment. "Well, of course they died out. What did they expect?" But the Shakers had never relied on reproduction to bring new members. Nuns and monks don't have children, either, and many Catholic convents and monasteries have lasted for well over a thousand years. But the rule of celibacy obviously made it harder to keep young Shakers loyal, and to attract new members.

Shakers had welcomed the World's unwanted children, and they had been a fruitful source of converts. But social customs were changing. Children now were seldom indentured as servants or apprentices. The Civil War had produced a large crop of orphans, but few foundlings arrived on Shaker doorsteps. More and more, government and private charities established institutions which took over the Shakers' paternal role.

Especially in the devastated South, the reasons for the decline were partly economic. The war had beggared thousands of formerly prosperous landowners, and this included the inhabitants of the two southernmost Shaker villages, Pleasant Hill and South Union.

During the war, both armies had stormed through Kentucky numerous times. The Shakers fed thousands of starving, battle-weary soldiers — Union or Confederate, it made no difference. Sometimes the Sisters set up tables in their front yards, and handed out food to exhausted men staggering by.

The soldiers "marched into our yards & surrounded our wells like the locusts of Egypt," wrote a Pleasant Hill Shaker, "and struggled with each other for the water as if perishing with thirst, and they thronged our kitchen doors and windows, begging for bread like hungry wolves, we nearly emptied our kitchens of their contents, and they tore the loaves and pies into fragments, and divided them as eagerly as if they were starving."[3]

The Shakers served meals to privates as well as to generals; they bound up wounds and buried the dead. Raiders from both armies relentlessly pillaged the Shakers' land. Eldress Nancy Moore of South Union wrote bitterly: "Some of them [Union soldiers] got into the sweet potatoes patch and grabbled about 100 hills. And of course they helped themselves to as many apples as they wanted . . . Frederick said his melon patch looked as tho' there had been 100 hogs in it . . . So we had soldiers East of us and West of us and rebels all around."[4]

Soon the resources of their villages dwindled, but the Shakers rarely charged for the food and care they gave. "We have uniformly refused any compensation . . . and they are lavish with their thanks for our hospitality."[5]

The southern villages had once been showplaces of prize-winning cattle and horses, famed for agricultural excellence. But after the war, their economy was in ruins, and membership dropped off rapidly. The once-flourishing enterprises never recovered from the strain.

❧

Up north, however, the Shaker economy was apparently thriving. Shakers marketed baskets, bonnets, wooden boxes, vegetable seeds, liver tonics, applesauce — they had dozens of irons in the fire. Chair-making continued to be one of their most lucrative enterprises. In 1853, the New Lebanon Brothers had turned out a mere 130 chairs; by 1860 they were up to 600 chairs a year.[6]

In 1863, the management of the chair industry was taken over by a talented entrepreneur, Robert Wagan, who had been a Shaker since his parents indentured him at the age of seven. "Br. Robert is enterprising," Henry Blinn remarked. "He says anything will sell that is carried into the market."[7] Under the guidance of the enterprising Brother Robert, business flourished. In 1872, the Shakers built a full-blown factory.

Henry Blinn was a fascinated visitor to the humming, clanging chairworks. He noted with a touch of awe that "the machinery in it has cost some $25,000 . . . They have an engine of 15 horsepower and a boiler of 20 horsepower. The whole building is heated by steam." This establishment was soon cranking out "two doz chairs per day . . . Already they have orders for more than they can furnish."[8]

But business, perhaps, was a little too successful. As workshops became factories, and handicrafts became industries, some Shakers began to get worried. The original impulse that had driven Shakerism, the desire to withdraw from the World to seek spiritual perfection, was in danger of being swamped by their growing commercial success. How could the Shakers withdraw from the sinful World — when the sinners were their loyal customers?

Commerce was booming in the World, as well. Shakers were not the only ones building factories. Soon shoddy machine-made goods were flooding the market, giving the Shaker enterprises a run for their money. In the "Gilded Age," there was less interest in the Shakers' superb craftsmanship and their legendary perfection. One by one, Shaker industries began to scale down, or close altogether.

Frederick Evans, always clear-sighted, noticed the handwriting on the wall. "We used to have more looms than now," he wrote sadly in 1875. "But cloth is sold so cheaply that we gradually began to buy. It is a mistake; we buy more cheaply than we can make, but our homemade cloth is much better than that we can buy; and we now have to make three pairs of trousers, for instance, where before we made one."[9]

Brothers continued to abandon the Society at an alarming rate. The Shakers now needed to hire help for almost every sort of men's work. No longer were there enough strong young Brethren to plow the fields, hoe the crops, or get in the hay. Henry Blinn wrote sadly, "A hired man has been engaged to drive the horses belonging to the office, and to do business between the Village and Concord. We had formerly, been able to furnish help from the family to do this work."[10] The New Lebanon chair factory, he wrote, employed "ten hands."[11]

The remaining Sisters, many elderly, often had unpleasant confrontations with rowdy, hard-drinking hired men who did not share the Shakers' ideals or understand their ways. Sometimes the conflicts between the Shakers and their employees grew violent. In 1875, Henry wrote bitterly that a disgruntled hired man had burned down two buildings at New Lebanon, including the Family Dwelling. The man was "sentenced to 14 years in the state prison."[12]

Perhaps the main reason for the Shakers' lessened enrollment was simply that the times were changing. The impassioned religious revivals of the eighteenth and early nineteenth centuries were over. It was an increasingly secular age. People spent less time agonizing over their sins, dreading the arrival of Judgment Day. Most folk, especially the young, were less concerned about the state of their souls and more interested in making their fortunes. Once, leaving home to join the Shakers had seemed a great adventure, an exciting quest to find God and discover one's own soul. Now, a new frontier was opening up — a physical frontier, not a spiritual one.

In the mid-1800s, a politician named George Henry Evans had led a land reform movement designed to make it possible for working men to acquire land and thereby gain economic independence. After many years of lobbying by Evans and other reformers, Abraham Lincoln had signed the Homestead Act of 1862, which bestowed 160 acres of public land on those who would venture west. Anyone 21 and older, including females or freed slaves, could file a claim, although no one who had borne arms against the government was eligible. The requirements were that homesteaders agree to farm the land for five years, and to build a house of at least 12-by-14-feet in size.

As soon as the Civil War was over, the Union Army was free to turn its attention to the Native Americans. Soon the frontier had been viciously "pacified," and Indian territories were open to settlement. Millions headed west to chase their dreams in what was the largest migration in American history.[13]

George Henry Evans is sometimes referred to as the father of the Homestead Act, although he died shortly before it was passed. His commitment to land reform was whole-heartedly shared by Frederick Evans, his beloved younger brother. But the idealistic brothers did not foresee some of the shortcomings of the Homestead Act. For one thing, 160 acres of arid western rangeland were barely enough to sustain a farm, and many settlers lost their shirts. Also, the Act was subject to much abuse, as big ranches and corporations took advantage of it to claim timber or oil-producing land, or file fraudulent claims to deny water rights to competing businesses.

Elder Frederick also did not foresee that the triumphant land reform movement was part of the death-knell of the Shakers. How could the Shakers keep their young men and women down on the farm, devoted to a tranquil life of work and worship, when adventure and riches were beckoning in the West?

In 1899, in the final days of the nineteenth century, Henry Blinn paid a visit to the Shaker village of Tyringham. This Massachusetts village, established in 1792, had a spectacular setting; the buildings clung to the sides of a steep mountain that towered above the green crop-fields on the valley floor. The barns, Dwelling House, Meeting House, and workshops were magnificent structures crafted with the Shakers' usual skill and care. Henry wrote, "Everywhere was to be seen the substantial work of consecrated hands."[14]

But the Dwelling House windows were dark; the Meeting House was silent. Owls roosted in the empty barns. Tyringham had closed in 1875, and Henry Blinn's visit was filled with sadness. The Shakers who had sung and danced and worked there were gone.

Canterbury Village, however, was very much alive. Henry Blinn lived the rest of his long life in the still-bustling village. Canterbury's membership was diminishing slowly, but many vigorous Brothers and Sisters remained.

Few mentions of the World's events obtrude in Henry's *Historical Record,* in which he incorporated journal entries with statistics and biographical notes. Generally, only a few paragraphs are devoted to each year. But in his entry for the day of his draft examination, he had written pages. He described the event in minute detail, the words flowing from his pen. Now that the war was over, the *Record* resumed a dry account of the Shakers' lives: debates over tea-drinking and the eating of "swine-flesh," statistics on eggs gathered and pounds of butter churned, and the daily business of the farm, Dwelling House, and school. It was as though he had closed his window on the World.

But Shaker life was still rich with interest and filled with possibilities. Henry busied himself with a host of tasks and pursuits, following enough careers for several lifetimes. Increasingly, he found solace in nature, and he studied and taught natural history. His interest in science grew, and he developed a small museum at Canterbury to house his geological specimens and other artifacts.

Henry was a born scientist, a precise observer and a meticulous keeper of records. He organized Shaker historical documents, tallied endless agricultural statistics, and described the specimens in his geological collection with records of their color, hardness, and shape. He noted the passing of Brothers and Sisters, recording fascinating details of their lives as well as their deaths.[15] Henry planted the first arboretum in New Hampshire, behind the Canterbury schoolhouse, so that the students could study botany. Tall trees still flourish there today. His print shop expanded, making Canterbury the publishing center for all the Shaker communities, and he was editor of *The Manifesto,* a beloved periodical which linked all the Shaker villages, offering agricultural advice, chatty news of friends, and inspirational articles. He wrote numerous books, one a tiny volume less than two inches square, full of nuggets of wisdom especially for children.

But as the years went by, Shaker membership continued to erode. With quiet desperation, Henry Blinn and other progressive Elders and Eldresses sought to modernize Shakerism. The old stern rules were relaxed. Novel-reading was allowed, where once all literature had been strictly controlled. Victorian curlicues were tacked on to austere New England buildings. Now Shakers could put flowers in vases, pictures on walls, fringes on tablecloths. Comfortable "settees [were] used at the Meeting House," instead of "long benches without backs."[16]

Music, the foundation of Shaker worship since Mother Ann sang out in her strong, clear voice, was changing too. Henry Blinn and Eldress Dorothy Durgin pioneered the use of musical instruments; Shaker-like, they were always willing to try new things, and introduced a pump-organ to Canterbury. Other instruments were soon allowed, for recreational use and eventually in worship services. The "studying of round notes," a means of musical notation, was "another radical departure," Henry wrote.[17]

In 1873, he traveled widely, visiting Shaker communities as far away as Kentucky and recording the changes he observed. It's hard to tell from his words whether he felt sadness or approval, as change after change swept in. The original Shaker ways were softened, relaxed, diluted, in the hope of attracting new converts and keeping the young faithful. But nothing could stop the tide.

❧

Frederick Evans remained the Shakers' most popular spokesman. His writings took on a monumentally biblical tone, and he penned *The Autobiography of a Shaker,* subtitled *The Revelation of the Apocalypse.* He toured Great Britain, lecturing on Shaker ways, and shocked standing-room-only audiences with his radical theological views, announcing that God was equally male and female, and marriage was not a Christian institution.

Elder Frederick passed away in 1893, after six decades as a Shaker. He would probably have agreed with the anonymous Shaker who wrote "Death is but taking off the coat."[18] Friends who shared his whole-hearted belief in spiritualism reported that they long afterwards felt his presence trying to communicate with them, but they were never able to make contact.[19]

Other Shakers, notably Evans's colleagues at Mount Lebanon including Catherine Allen, Antoinette Doolittle, and Daniel Offord, continued his work of social reform. As the twentieth century rolled around, the Shakers became ever more deeply involved in the World's problems. "No citizen is more thoroughly alive to the interests of state or nation than are the Shakers," declared Sister Anna White. "In the Peace of the nation is our Peace."[20] The Shakers no longer attempted to live withdrawn from the sinful World. Now many saw it as their duty to help make the World a better place. Shaker reformers were in the forefront of the early movements for the rights and welfare of children, civil rights, and women's suffrage.

The humane treatment of animals had always been a concern of the Shakers, whose earliest laws forbade cruel or unnecessary beating of animals. Now as the rest of the world caught up to them, they continued their commitment. They joined the fledgling Audubon Society in deploring the "slaughter of little birds," referring to the massacres of songbirds that took place at Christmas, as well as the trade in feathers for ladies' hats that sacrificed millions of birds. An article in the Shaker newsletter about the Spanish-American War expressed pity for the Spanish soldiers as well as "great sorrow for the sufferings inflicted on our own soldiers and on our army horses and mules, to large numbers of whom death has been a happy release."[21]

And they continued their unswerving commitment to pacifism. In 1905, less than a decade before the horrible bloodbath of World War I, the New Lebanon Shakers sponsored a "Peace Convention." The participants adopted a resolution which declared that "wars are equally barbarous and equally unnecessary . . . a return to primitive savagery."[22] The Peace Convention called for not only worldwide arms reduction, but the creation of an international tribunal, strong enough to arbitrate disputes between nations and ensure the world's peace.

Following in Frederick Evans's footsteps, Eldress Anna White (Figure 12) and Sister Sarah Burger of New Lebanon paid a call on the president at the White House to hand-deliver the resolutions passed by the Peace Convention. In what must surely have been an interesting meeting, the white-bonneted, stern-eyed Eldress urged Theodore Roosevelt to work for world peace and disarmament.

Figure 12. A contemporary of Elder Frederick Evans, Eldress Anna White carried on his role of advocate for peace. Her meeting with Theodore Roosevelt was described as "Turk meets Turk." Use courtesy of Shaker Museum and Library, Old Chatham and New Lebanon, NY.

Like Lincoln, Roosevelt heard the Shakers out with courtesy. "His eyes never wavered from the face of this Shaker Eldress of seventy-five years, nor did her gaze flinch from his steady, piercing look. It was, as someone quaintly observed, Turk meet Turk."[23]

The president answered respectfully that he did not feel that disarmament was practicable. "Justice before peace!" he insisted. The resolutions were left "in the hands of a committee and were afterward incorporated in the work of the Hague Tribunal."[24]

Once again, the Shakers were ahead of their times. They foresaw, though they could not prevent, the world wars of the twentieth century, whose casualty lists would dwarf those of the War Between the States.

༄

Henry Blinn saw many changes during his long life. Born in horse-and-buggy days, he lived to see the first automobiles cruising the New Hampshire landscape. As the twentieth century opened, he was an elder statesman among the Shakers, much beloved (Figure 13).

"Gradually, gracefully, he seemed to outgrow the responsibilities of earth." His health began to fail, and he moved into apartments in the Infirmary, though he was "never better pleased than when able to spend the day at his carpenter's bench." But after "two slight shocks, which foreshadowed the end, he seemed to lose control of the right hand; and quietly passed the choice pens, which he had used for so many years, to his younger friends as gifts, saying, 'I cannot use them now.'"

He "followed the rounds of the day, blessing and being blessed, until the week preceding his demise. The last Wednesday of his life, in answer to the query, 'Are you tired, Elder Henry?' he gently answered, 'O, well, there is rest for the weary.'"[25] Finally, he "opened the door to Life Eternal," as the Shakers put it, and passed peacefully away in 1905, sixty-seven years a Shaker.

༄

Figure 13. "Gradually, gracefully, he seemed to outgrow the responsibilities of earth. The last Wednesday of his life, in answer to the query, 'Are you tired, Elder Henry?' he gently answered, 'O, well, there is rest for the weary.'" Use courtesy of Shaker Museum and Library, Old Chatham and New Lebanon, NY.

Perhaps part of Elder Henry's weariness was caused by his fear that the decline of Shakerism was irreversible. The communities had been joyfully "gathered into order" one by one, in the eighteenth and nineteenth centuries. Now, in the twentieth century, they were closing, one by one. Village after village shut down due to lack of members: Shirley, Massachusetts, in 1908; Pleasant Hill in 1910; Harvard in 1918, South Union in 1922; Alfred, Maine, in 1932. The grim progression was impossible to halt. Watervliet was Mother Ann's original settlement, and the site of her grave, but it was abandoned in 1938. The seat of the Central Ministry, powerful Mount Lebanon itself, closed down in 1947.

In the sadness and chaos of the closings, much was lost. Priceless antiques and historical records were sold or thrown on the junk pile. Sister Lucy Bowers of Enfield, Connecticut, watched as "Over one hundred books called 'Sacred Roll,' 'Divine Book of Holy Wisdom,' and others are thrown out of the attic window and burned."[26] Chairs or tables that today might sell for thousands of dollars were given away, or burned as trash.

Aging Sisters, unable to cope with heavy chores, sadly sold their tools and livestock. Sister Lucy vividly described the closing of the once-thriving Enfield dairy operation. "Three teams and eight men come to take the cows away" she wrote in sad resignation. "Cows are wild, run in every direction." The big barns stood empty. "One remaining cow is taken by the Polanders at the west after dinner," Sister Lucy remembered bitterly. "The last distressing scene so far as our cows are concerned, for she had to be pulled every inch of the way."[27]

When a village closed, the remaining Sisters moved in with aging Sisters in other villages. A few elderly ladies now lived in the big Dwelling Houses, using only two or three of the silent rooms. Sister Mary Dahm, who had relocated to Hancock from Watervliet, wrote in a letter to a friend. "The sisters are very kind but this dark house is very depressing to an already broken heart. [T]he hills smother me and this room crushes me." Not even another Shaker village was the same as the place where she had lived so happily. "Home is where the heart is," she wrote sadly, "and mine is not here."[28]

Notes

[1] Patterson, *Shaker Spiritual*, p. 373. This most beloved and famous of all Shaker songs was made by Elder Joseph Brackett. In modern times the lovely melody has reappeared in many guises, from a symphony to a car commercial. "Simple Gifts" was heard by millions around the globe when it was played by Yo-Yo Ma, Itzhak Perlman, Anthony McGill, and Gabriela Montero at the inauguration of Barack Obama on January 20, 2009.

[2] Garrett, Clarke. *From the Old World to the New World: Origins of the Shakers*. Baltimore, MD: Johns Hopkins University Press, 1987, p. 236.

[3] Clark, *Pleasant Hill in the Civil War*, p. 38.

[4] Moore, Nancy. *The Journal of Eldress Nancy Moore*. Mary Julia Neal, editor. Nashville, TN: The Parthenon Press, 1963, p. 226.

[5] Clark, *Pleasant Hill in the Civil War*, p. 46.

[6] Muller and Rieman, *Shaker Chair*, p. 169.

[7] Ibid.

[8] Ibid., p. 170.

[9] Melcher, Marguerite. *The Shaker Adventure. A History of the Shakers from the Eighteenth Century to the Twentieth*. Old Chatham, NY: The Shaker Museum, 1986, p. 179.

[10] Blinn, *Record*, vol. 1, p. 180.

[11] Muller and Rieman, *Shaker Chair*, p. 170.

[12] Blinn, *Record*, vol. 1, p. 233.

[13] Bowen, ed., *This Fabulous Century*, p. 78.

[14] Blinn, "Notes From our Diary," September 1, 1899, *The Manifesto*, November 1899, pp. 248–253.

[15] Blinn, *Record*, vol. 2, p. 232. Henry Blinn recorded in detail the fascinating lives of some Brothers or Sisters before they joined the Shakers, including, for example, the saga of a Sister who as a child was captured by Indians and held for ransom for her weight in silver.

[16] Blinn, *Record*, vol. 1, p. 224.

[17] Ibid., p. 229.

[18] Sprigg, *By Shaker Hands*, p. 19.

[19] Stein, *Shaker Experience*, p. 321.

[20] Ibid., p. 317.

[21] *The Manifesto*, February 1899, vol. 29, no. 2, p. 32.

[22] Stein, Shaker Experience, p. 317.

[23] Taylor, *A Memorial to Eldress Anna White*, p. 79.

[24] Ibid.

[25] *Memoriam*, p. 39.

[26] Burns, *Shaker Cities*, p. 186.

[27] Ibid., p. 185.

[28] Stein, *Shaker Experience*, p. 349.

Epilogue

Remembered As a Chair

On Zion's hill is clearly seen,
By souls who do not live unclean,
The tree of life, forever green...
Establish'd by the Lord's command,
This tree will there forever stand.

— Shaker hymn[1]

The bell on top of the Canterbury Dwelling House has a rich, sweet chime that echoes over the whole village. Made by the famous Revere Bellworks, the five-hundred-pound bell woke the Brothers and Sisters in the morning, calling them to meals, work, and worship year after year. It was the heartbeat of the village. As the twentieth century opened, the deep tones of the bell were joined by another, shriller sound — the ringing of a telephone.

The pace of change was accelerating at light speed, and the Shakers were not afraid of it. They had always embraced technology. Telephones were installed at Canterbury in 1901. Electricity was slow in coming to rural areas, but the Shakers didn't sit around and wait for it. In 1910 they constructed a powerhouse which contained a gasoline-powered generator to make their own electricity and light sixteen of their buildings. Brother Irving Greenwood learned the electrician's trade, and supervised installation of lights and outlets; it took years for the rest of the region to catch up with them. The Shakers long remembered the magic of the first night the village was illuminated with electric lights.

The Canterbury community's first car, acquired in 1907, was an elegant REO Speedwagon. By 1918, the Sisters no longer used a horse-drawn wagon to go apple-picking — they rode to the orchard in a roomy pick-up truck. Canterbury Shakers used sewing machines, typewriters, a radio, cameras, a motorized ice cream maker. There were even rumors that the Shakers were planning on buying an airplane. While they never went this far, they did take to the skies earlier than most Americans. Brother Irving Greenwood flew to Chicago in 1933.

No more did they withdraw from the World. Now, Shakers took vacations. No more were there tight restrictions on travel, or rules against mingling with the World's people; Shakers went to the zoo, visited friends in cities, or enjoyed the seaside. Outsiders still visited the Shakers, but not to watch their exuberant singing and dancing worship. Public services became more and more infrequent and in some villages disappeared completely.[2]

So in the modern age, it was easier to be a Shaker — but also harder. Bereft of the many strong hands that had run the workshops and made their farms and barns into agricultural showplaces, the Shakers were facing hard times. It was decided, for economic reasons, to stop publishing *The Manifesto*, in 1899. The lively periodical was sorely missed. Now, each shrinking village was more isolated than ever.

There were fewer than a thousand Shakers by 1900. In some villages, money was tight; in others, aging members confronted the threat of real poverty. In place of the booming industries, elderly Sisters worked hard making fancy goods and knick-knacks for sale to tourists. As the World's interest in Shaker antiques grew, some villages sold off classic pieces of furniture to the eager dealers. Eldress Emma B. King wrote "The old-time relics are dear to us and only the immediate need of money would induce us to part with them."[3] An irritated Sister snapped, "Those people would grab the chairs right out from under us if we'd let them."[4]

The decline in membership steepened. Dozens remained, where once there were thousands. Most of the villages had closed. By 1950, the Shakers were down to about forty members.

In 1960, three remaining Sisters lived in the five-story brick Dwelling House at Hancock, Massachusetts. The famous Round Barn was on the verge of collapse. Huge, ugly cracks weakened the gracefully curved stone walls, so that they had to be propped in place by heavy beams. The Central Ministry arranged for the property to be sold to a not-for-profit group and turned into a museum.

As the turbulent decade of the Sixties opened, only two Shaker villages remained: Canterbury, New Hampshire, and Sabbathday Lake, Maine.

∾

The large dining hall at Sabbathday Lake Shaker Village is, to this day, a sunny, pleasant room. For many decades, it accommodated large numbers of people. In traditional Shaker fashion, males sat on one side of the room, females on the other, as the long rows of diners ate their meals at the polished wooden tables in appreciative silence. In 1960, the few remaining Shakers at the Maine village still ate in the big dining hall: Sisters on one side of the room, and on the other, the sole remaining male Shaker, Brother Delmer Wilson, in solitary state at his own table.

After the death of Brother Delmer in 1961, Shakerism became a wholly female institution. And an elderly one; most young Sisters had abandoned the Shaker life. As the nineteenth century had moved into the twentieth, more career opportunities beckoned females; society slowly became more accepting of single women who sought a role other than that of wife and mother. And like the Brothers, fewer Sisters were willing to bear the cross of celibacy.

But some women loyally stayed. The Shaker life still offered women the opportunity for freedom, companionship, and creativity. But no new Sisters arrived, and the Sisterhood was inevitably aging.

They weren't sour old maids mourning the old days, though. Many friends and neighbors in the World remember the fun and joyousness that prevailed during the last years of Canterbury. The remaining New Hampshire Sisters continued the trend of liberalizing the Shaker way. They listened to the radio, put on plays, had parties. They not only allowed instrumental music in worship, they started their own band, witnessed by a photograph of two caped and bonneted Sisters, each proudly holding a gleaming saxophone.

And then, the diminishing Shaker Sisterhood made a discovery — they found, to their astonishment, that they were rich.

As communities closed, the Shakers had sold many parcels of land for thousands of dollars. In addition, several shrewd Trustees had put their funds into railroads, bonds and securities, electric utilities and other solid investments.[5] Years of thrift added to the revenues from the sale of properties. Since 1929, their assets had been held in a trust fund, and the remaining Believers were, apparently, unaware of just how large these assets were. In 1957, Eldress Emma B. King was "stunned to learn that the United Society controlled about a million dollars worth of holdings."[6]

∽

In 1965, a surprising decision was made by Eldress Emma King of Canterbury, and Eldress Gertrude Soule of Sabbathday Lake. These two leaders, the remnants of the Central Ministry, decided to close the ranks of Shakerdom to new members.

Once the Shakers had put benches for the public in their Meeting Houses, hoping to lure converts; they had endured the World's mockery and persecution for the sake of attracting newcomers. It's unclear, to this day, why the Eldresses reached this decision. One possible reason was the fear that false converts would be attracted by the Shakers' considerable financial assets, like the "bread-and-butter" Shakers of old.[7]

It seemed, then, that the future of Shakerism was clear. The last few Sisters would gradually pass away, and Shakers would become as extinct as dinosaurs.

But something unexpected happened. A new convert, a scholar and historian named Theodore Johnson, wished to join the Shakers. The question of his admission precipitated a controversy that shook the now-tiny Shaker world. While the Sisters in Canterbury stuck to their resolve not to accept new members, the Sabbathday Lake community accepted him. Over the years, other new converts, both Brothers and Sisters, have followed. As of this writing the Sabbathday Lake community has four Shakers.

 ∽

Canterbury, New Hampshire, gets a lot of snow. I visited the research library at the Shaker village one cold February morning, as the flakes sifted down. On the snowy paths, no footsteps but mine marred the fresh whiteness. Drifts were piled high around the silent Dwelling House, where no faces looked out of the many windows to see what the weather was doing. Almost all the buildings are painted white now, in contrast to the bright hues of Henry Blinn's day. The empty village was as quiet as a ghost.

By 1974, there were about the same number of Shakers as when the loyal handful arrived from England, two hundred years before. In the closing years of the twentieth century, the last Shaker Sisters at Canterbury passed away one by one, loved and lamented by many. They continued the Shaker tradition of loving care of children. Darryl Thompson, who grew up living near the Shakers and knew them well, speaks with deep affection and respect of his "thirteen grandmothers."[8] Ethel Hudson, the last Canterbury Shaker, died in 1992, at the age of 96. Canterbury is a magnificent museum now, a beautiful, empty shell.

But the Sabbathday Lake Shakers are still very much alive. The "blessed fire" of the Shaker way of life has stretched a long way through time and space, from Ann Lee's beginnings in Toad Lane, Manchester, to this New England farm. With a stubbornness that rivals Mother Ann's, the Shakers have persisted.

Their once-remote Maine site is no longer isolated from civilization. The wide fields and lovely buildings have been threatened by development. The Shakers joined hands with the Trust for Public Land, Maine Preservation, and other environmental organizations to obtain conservation easements to protect the landscape and seventeen historic buildings. The 1,700-acre property has received the prestigious National Preservation Honor Award from the National Trust for Historic Preservation. Nowadays, Sabbathday Lake Shaker Village receives thousands of visitors every year.

All kinds of people make the pilgrimage. Some seek spiritual refreshment. Others are delighted by the beauty of Shaker crafts, the baskets and oval boxes, light as a feather and built to last for centuries. Nature-lovers enjoy the green meadows and open spaces. Families bring their kids to see the rustic barns and pet the animals, and historians come to use the excellent research library. Shaker fans take guided tours with the eager curiosity of passengers on a whale-watch, hoping to glimpse a real live Shaker.

But if you can't make the long journey all the way up to Maine, just Google "Sabbathday Lake" for a virtual visit. True to the Shakers' abiding love of technology, Sabbathday Lake Village has an elegant and well-designed website.[9] The Shakers' traditional excellent products, including rosewater and a variety of herbal teas, can now be ordered on-line.

The current Shakers don't know what the future may bring, but they don't plan to become dinosaurs. "God will provide," Sister Frances Carr, a twenty-first-century Shaker, writes cheerfully. "She always has."[10]

~

As I leave the Shaker Dwelling House, I take a last look at the lamp that hangs from the ceiling of the wide hallway. Once again, I admire the well-designed ventilation pipe that cleanses the air of soot and smoke, protecting health while efficiently lighting the hall. Like the Shakers' chairs, the lamp is superbly designed for its function.

But the Shakers are about so much more than furniture. Antique collectors have hounded the Shakers for almost a century, but most people are uninterested in, or unaware of, the rich history and passionate religion of the folk who created the beautiful cabinets, benches, and tables. Sister Mildred Barker spoke for many of her fellow Believers when she cried bitterly "I don't want to be remembered as a piece of furniture!"[11]

Chairs are far from being the Shakers' only legacy. Their beliefs helped to shape the young American nation. Shakers led the way in women's rights and civil rights. They were among the first Americans to concern themselves with the defenseless and to speak for the voiceless, working for children's welfare and the humane treatment of animals.

Shakers pioneered medical and dietary reforms, championing causes that only became popular in modern times. Their warnings on the dangers of germs, alcohol, poor nutrition, and smoking turned out to be right on the money. Shakers could arguably be called the first American environmentalists; their eccentric insistence on pure water and clean air doesn't sound quite so crazy today. With the planet groaning under the weight of more than six billion people, even celibacy doesn't seem like such a bad idea.

But it was the Shakers' unwavering commitment to pacifism and non-violence that is perhaps their most enduring contribution. Shaker thought influenced Ralph Waldo Emerson, Bronson Alcott, and Leo Tolstoy. Their ideals were well-known to Henry David Thoreau when he wrote *Civil Disobedience,* and through him the Shakers can claim to have influenced Gandhi and Martin Luther King.

In spite of Sister Mildred's acid remark, it is true that Shakers are often "remembered as a chair." They might have faded into historical oblivion, along with communities like the Harmonists or the Perfectionists, if not for their genius in craftsmanship, their artistry and their commitment to perfection. Their legacy of beauty is there for us to see and touch, in each remaining building, each surviving basket, oval box, and piece of furniture. In a way, a perfectly-crafted chair is an appropriate symbol of the Shakers.

But when I think back to my first encounter with these strange Believers, I always remember the lamp, shining in the Dwelling House hallway; I see the flame glowing brightly in the clean air. So many of the inventions and ideals of the Shakers preceded those of the World; in so many ways, they lit up the darkness, and showed us the way. So perhaps, instead of a chair, the Shakers would prefer to be remembered as a lamp.

––––––––

Notes

[1] Goodwillie, *Shaker Songs,* p. 29. An early hymn, ca. 1812. The words are attributed to Richard McNemar.

[2] Stein, *Shaker Experience,* p. 298.

[3] Ibid., p. 395.

[4] Kirk, John T. *The Shaker World: Art, Life, Belief.* New York, NY: Harry N. Abrams, Inc., 1997, p. 243.

[5] Stein, *Shaker Experience,* p. 275.

[6] Sprigg, June. *Simple Gifts; Lessons in Living From a Shaker Village.* New York, NY: Vintage Books, 1998, p. 77.

[7] Ibid., p. 74.

[8] Darryl Thompson, personal communication, September, 2007.

[9] See *www.shaker.lib.me.us,* the website of Sabbathday Lake Shaker Village.

[10] Cohen, *Simple Gifts,* p. 10.

[11] Morse, *Shakers and the World's People,* p. 240.

Shaker Sites

Shaker sites are scattered across the eastern United States (Figure 14). The locations of the earliest villages mark the route of Ann Lee's travels as she moved from Albany, New York, across the Berkshires and through New England. Some of these sites, like Harvard and Shirley, mark spots where Mother Ann and her followers confronted hostile mobs or suffered beatings and abuse.

Before Mother Ann's death, she predicted that the next "great work of the Lord" would be in the west. Accordingly, the Shakers, always looking to spread the faith, turned their eyes to the western frontier. Early in the nineteenth century, missionaries established settlements in the wilderness lands of Ohio, Indiana, and Kentucky.

As the nineteenth century opened, village after village was "gathered into order" as converts flocked. Shaker membership peaked in the 1830s, at about 6,000 Brothers and Sisters. Then a steady downturn began, and villages began to close.

Later, at the end of the nineteenth century, ageing Believers began to consider the advantages of a warmer climate. Tired of the bitter winters of upstate New York, some Shakers bought land down south, and turned their hands to raising pineapples and bananas.

As their membership numbers declined, the Shakers razed or sold buildings rather than allow them to become dilapidated. Some properties were sold to private owners, some to religious groups, and others to state governments to be turned into schools, homes for the elderly, or prisons.[1]

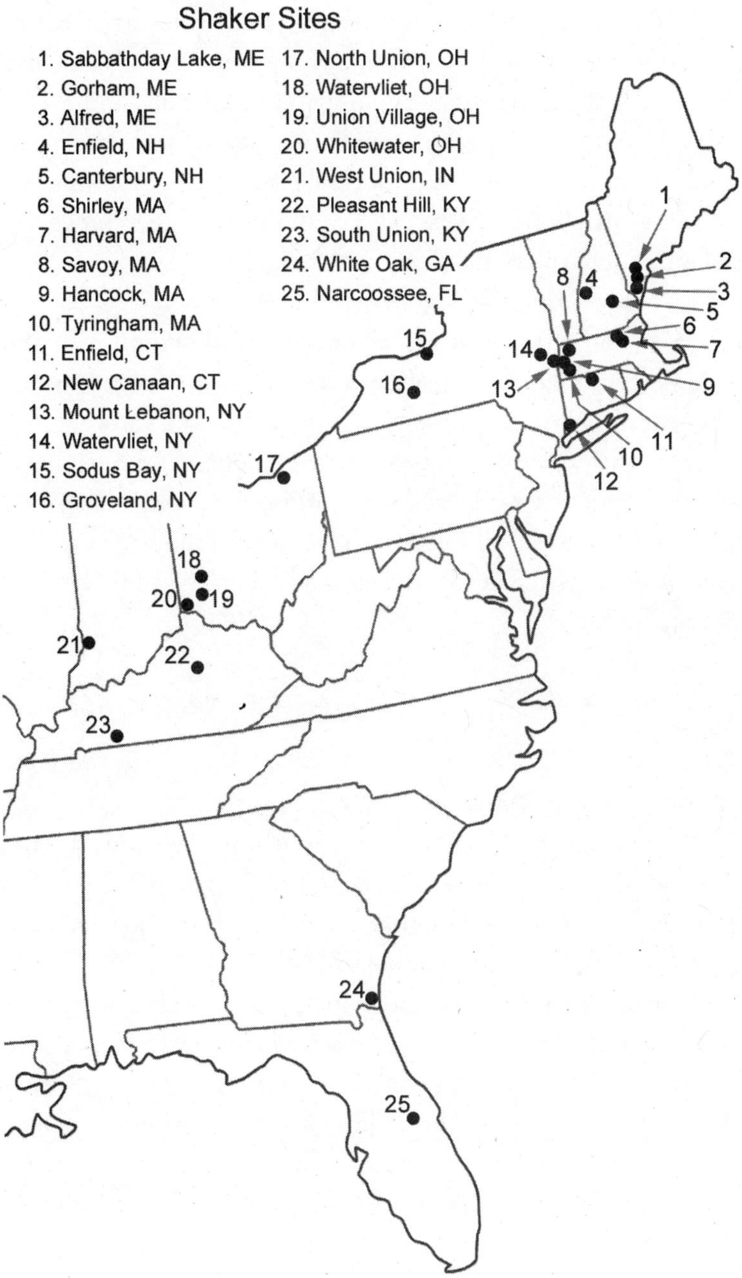

Shaker Sites

1. Sabbathday Lake, ME
2. Gorham, ME
3. Alfred, ME
4. Enfield, NH
5. Canterbury, NH
6. Shirley, MA
7. Harvard, MA
8. Savoy, MA
9. Hancock, MA
10. Tyringham, MA
11. Enfield, CT
12. New Canaan, CT
13. Mount Lebanon, NY
14. Watervliet, NY
15. Sodus Bay, NY
16. Groveland, NY
17. North Union, OH
18. Watervliet, OH
19. Union Village, OH
20. Whitewater, OH
21. West Union, IN
22. Pleasant Hill, KY
23. South Union, KY
24. White Oak, GA
25. Narcoossee, FL

Figure 14. A map of known Shaker sites. The Believers spread the gospel and established villages in the eastern United States from Maine to Florida.

None of the Shaker settlements offered Believers an easy life, especially in their early days. Some of the communities lasted only a few years, their bright hopes fading amid tensions and disagreements. Wars, fires, drought, famine, even earthquakes and plagues of locusts took their toll. But several Shaker communities lasted for more than a hundred years — Canterbury endured for two hundred and Sabbathday Lake Shaker Village will mark its 215th anniversary in 2009 and is still going strong.

A few of these historic places are now magnificent living history sites, open to the public, with state-of-the-art museums, libraries, and interpretive programs. Some sites are works-in-progress, with exciting plans for development. At others, nothing remains but the barest traces of foundations — and memories. An annotated listing of all known Shaker sites follows, as well as a description of the Shaker Museum and Library and The Shaker Historic Trail.

∽

MAINE

Alfred — *Alfred, Maine; 1793–1932*

Alfred was the first Shaker site in Maine. Woodworking, textiles, and fertile fields made Alfred a thriving community. According to tradition, it was here that Elder Joseph Brackett composed the famous Shaker song "Simple Gifts."

The community faced economic hard times in the twentieth century, and the few remaining Alfred Shakers left for Sabbathday Lake in 1931. The site was taken over by the Brothers of Christian Instruction, and many of the buildings are well preserved. There is a designated Alfred Shaker Historic District in the town and there are plans to restore some of the buildings and open them to the public.

Sabbathday Lake — *New Gloucester, Maine; 1794–present*

Sabbathday Lake is the only site that still has a community of practicing Shakers. Although located on Route 26, a well-traveled highway, the beautiful village still maintains a sense of isolation and serenity. The Shakers have worked with environmental organizations to obtain conservation easements to protect woodlands, fields, and seventeen historic buildings. The 1,700-acre property has received the prestigious National Preservation Honor Award from the National Trust for Historic Preservation. The site is a National Historic Landmark.

A museum is open to the public Memorial Day through Columbus Day, and there is a store where the Shakers sell hand-made goods and herbal products, as they have for so many years. Most of the buildings are accessible by guided tour only, and visitors are asked to respect the privacy of the Shakers. The research library, with a vast collection of resources on Shakers and non-mainstream religions, is open year round by appointment. The museum and store are open free of charge to all, but are closed on Sundays. An extensive program of special events, crafts workshops, and craft demonstrations are offered during the museum season.

Information about Sabbathday Lake and its museum, library, and supportive friends group is available on two websites: *http://www.shaker.lib.me.us* and *http://www.maineshakers.com*.

Gorham — *Gorham, Maine; 1808–1819*

Gorham was a short-lived Shaker site, a small village located halfway between Sabbathday Lake and Alfred which once had as many as fifty residents. However, soon after being established, members of this community merged with other Maine Shakers. Only a few buildings remain, and they are not open to the public.

NEW HAMPSHIRE

Canterbury — *Canterbury, New Hampshire; 1792–1992*

The view from Canterbury is still as lovely today as it was when Henry Blinn looked out over the broad New Hampshire countryside. The memory of the Shakers is kept vividly alive at this fascinating site, which has thirty buildings on almost 700 acres, as well as gardens, ponds, and woods. The great bell on top of the Dwelling House still rings out during tours. Visitors can see rooms in the Dwelling House preserved as they were when the last Canterbury Sisters lived there, and also restored buildings of earlier times, including a lovingly recreated classroom in the schoolhouse. The trees have grown tall in Henry Blinn's arboretum, the first in New Hampshire.

The Great Barn at Canterbury, built in 1856, was once the largest barn in New Hampshire. The immense structure, two hundred and fifty feet long, tragically burned to the ground in 1973, but to this day you can see huge foundation blocks, three feet high, skillfully fitted together like the masonry of an ancient Greek temple: a massive monument to the Shakers' architectural skills.

Spring to fall, the village is open for tours and offers a wide range of educational programs. Canterbury Shaker Village is a National Historic Landmark. Additional information about Canterbury is available at *http://www.shakers.org.*

Enfield — *Enfield, New Hampshire; 1793–1923*

Called "Chosen Vale" by the Shakers, Enfield Shaker Village is located in a scenic valley between Mascoma Lake and Mount Assurance. Enfield was famous for the Great Stone Dwelling House, once the tallest building north of Boston. The Shakers here owned 3,000 acres, and were known for their medicinal herb and seed-packaging industries.

When enrollment dwindled, the Shakers sold the land to the Catholic order of Our Lady of La Salette in the 1920s, after turning down a lucrative offer from a developer. A religious mission was founded on the site, and many new buildings were added. A nonprofit organization owns much of the settlement now, and there is a museum as well as many restored buildings, herb and flower gardens, and spectacular views of the New Hampshire countryside. Additional information about Enfield is available at *http://www.shakermuseum.org.*

MASSACHUSETTS

Hancock Shaker Village — *Pittsfield, Massachusetts; 1790–1960*

The lovely Hancock Shaker Village is now a living history museum. The five-story Brick Dwelling and many other buildings are stocked with fine examples of Shaker furniture, artifacts, and inventions. The big basement kitchen has enormous soup kettles and ingenious, labor-saving kitchen utensils. The 1858 water-powered turbine is demonstrated periodically, and its force still makes the Laundry & Machine Shop shudder. The much-photographed Round Stone Barn has been a tourist attraction since it was first built in the nineteenth century.

The last Hancock Sisters left in 1960, and the property was sold to a concerned group of local citizens and Shaker enthusiasts. The village opened to the public in 1961, with fascinating exhibits and interpretive displays. The big barns house historic breeds of livestock, and there are colorful gardens and nature trails. The village's main season is April to October, when there are many festivals, workshops, and special events, but tours are offered year-round. Hancock was designated a National Historic Landmark in 1968. Additional information about Hancock Shaker Village is available at *http://www.hancockshakervillage.org.*

Harvard — *Harvard, Massachusetts; 1791–1918*

Harvard was one of the first Shaker communities. Mother Ann made many converts in this area, but the local people were angered by the Shakers' unorthodox beliefs, and violent mobs persecuted the Shakers here. A marble shaft called the "Whipping Stone" still stands to mark the spot where James Whittaker and other Shakers were harassed and brutally flogged.

Despite the early difficulties, the Harvard community endured and eventually prospered. Shakers drained the surrounding marshlands to create fertile farm fields, and by the 1850s Harvard was a busy community with about 200 members working more than 2,000 acres.

Most of the members left after the Civil War, and the population was down to fewer than 40 at the turn of the century. Many of the Harvard community's buildings were sold to local residents, but historian Clara Endicott Sears purchased the 1794 office building and moved it to the nearby Fruitlands Museum, where it can be seen today.

There is a Shaker Historic District in the town of Harvard, but the buildings are not open to the public. Harvard Shaker Village Cemetery is the last resting place of many Harvard Shakers. The Fruitlands Museum houses Shaker artifacts, including "Mother Ann's chair."

Tyringham — *Tyringham, Massachusetts; 1792–1875*

Tyringham, beautifully situated on the side of a hill, was one of the earliest Shaker villages. It once had an immense maple-sugaring operation where Shakers tapped thousands of trees to make tons of the sweet syrup and sugar, a skill the early settlers learned from Native Americans. The Shakers blocked nearby streams to provide turbine power for their numerous machines, mills, and a broom factory.

As with most Shaker communities, the membership plummeted after the Civil War. The land and buildings were sold to local residents and the remaining Shakers went to live at other communities. Tyringham was the first eastern Shaker village to close.

Several Shaker buildings remain in the Tyringham Shaker Settlement Historic District, but they are privately owned and not open to the public. The Appalachian Trail passes through this scenic village and foundations of Shaker buildings can be seen along the trail.

Shirley — *Shirley, Massachusetts; 1793–1908*

Ann Lee visited the town of Shirley on her missionary journey and made many converts here. As at other locations, hostile mobs pursued her and threatened the Shakers with brutal violence. But by 1790, a community of worshippers was gathered, and they formally made a covenant as Shakers in 1793.

Shakers here ran several successful enterprises, and were well-known for their broom-making. Fragrant orchards provided apples for a booming applesauce business. Shirley Shakers reached their peak in the 1850s with more than a hundred members.

But by the twentieth century, the community had dwindled to only three remaining Sisters. The Shakers sold the land and buildings to the State of Massachusetts, which opened a reform school for boys on the property. After that school closed, the state developed correctional facilities on the site. Eleven of the original nineteenth-century Shaker buildings remain. The prison authorities limit visits, but it is possible to make special arrangements for guided tours of the Shaker site through the Shirley Historical Society.

The website of the Shirley Historical Society, *http://www.shirleyhistory.org/,* has information on Shirley Shaker Village and guided tours of the Shaker buildings.

Savoy — *Savoy, Massachusetts; 1817–1825*

Savoy is in the rocky hills of the Berkshire Mountains in western Massachusetts. Nothing now remains of this Shaker community but cellar holes and the remains of building foundations.

The site had a strange beginning. According to Shaker tradition, a woman arrived one day at Mount Lebanon and asked some Shaker Sisters for food. While she ate, she told them of a religious revival that was occurring in the mountainous region near Savoy, but said that the people were in need of guidance. "Throughout the interview she seemed careful that her face should not be seen and the sisters did not obtain a good look at her features. Rising at last and passing out, they watched her from the door; she walked unsteadily and suddenly, while they were looking at her, vanished from sight. They decided that they had been feeding and conversing with a spirit."[2]

Shaker missionaries soon found followers in the little mountain town, and they established a good-sized community of about eighty Shakers on 1,500 acres. But the rocky, hilly land made farming difficult, a plague of locusts hit their agricultural enterprises hard, and the undertaking failed to thrive. The Savoy Shakers were soon dispersed to other sites, although some returned and are buried in the area.

CONNECTICUT

Enfield — *Enfield, Connecticut; 1790–1917*

Enfield is located in northcentral Connecticut. Joseph Meacham, the Shakers' first American-born leader, came from this small town, and Mother Ann visited here several times, although — when they did so — she and her followers were frequently threatened by rioters.

Enfield was among the earliest Shaker settlements. It grew to be a prosperous village with nearly 100 buildings where, at its peak in the 1850s, approximately 200 members maintained a thriving seed business and an enormous dairy herd on 3,000 acres. Ironically, the Shaker community was not far from the town of Enfield's huge gunpowder factory, where much of the powder used by the Union in the Civil War was made.

By the turn of the century, enrollment at Enfield had declined, as was happening at all Shaker villages. After the last Believers departed, the state purchased the land and turned it into the Osborn State Prison Farm, using the dairy operation to provide vocational training to prisoners. A few Shaker buildings remain, some still owned by the prison, some privately owned, but none is open to the public.

Note that the Enfield, Connecticut, Shaker community should not be confused with the one at Enfield, New Hampshire.

New Canaan — *New Canaan, Connecticut; 1810–1812*

New Canaan, Connecticut, was a short-lived Shaker community of the early nineteenth century. This site is now a housing development and nothing Shaker remains. New Canaan came into being during a time of optimism and rapid expansion for the Shakers. However, few Connecticut folk converted, and the ground was rocky and hard to work. Stephan Fitch, a new convert, sold the Shakers the land for the site, but then had a series of acrimonious disagreements with his new Brethren. The community dissolved almost before it had begun.

NEW YORK

Watervliet — *Colonie, New York; 1787–1938*

Watervliet, now a suburb of Albany, was once a wilderness of forests and wetlands. Here Mother Ann's loyal followers built log cabins and laid up supplies for the converts that she predicted would come. Later, a thriving Shaker village stood here. Today, much of the flat farmland has been converted into Albany International Airport, and planes land and take off above the remaining Shaker buildings.

A non-profit group called the Shaker Heritage Society works to preserve the Watervliet Shaker Historic District, which is listed on the National Register of Historic Places. America's first Shaker settlement still has many buildings as well as open fields and an apple orchard. Mother Ann is buried in the Shaker cemetery, and visitors often leave a coin or a bright-colored pebble by her headstone. Nature trails lead around Ann Lee pond. There is a small museum, and some of the buildings are open to the public. Tours and programs are available. Note that this site is located in the town of Colonie, New York. Town boundaries have changed over two centuries, and the modern town of Watervliet is several miles away.

Additional information about the Shaker Heritage Society and Watervliet is available at *http://www.shakerheritage.org*.

Mount Lebanon — *New Lebanon, New York; 1787–1947*

Mount Lebanon, often called "New Lebanon" before the Civil War, was the Shakers' center of power, the seat of the Central Ministry. This enormous community was both a spiritual and administrative hub, the "Vatican" of the Shakers. There were once six hundred members and more than a hundred buildings on 6,000 acres.

Many historic structures still stand, although the stone dairy barn, the largest in America, was tragically gutted by a fire in 1972. Known as the Great Stone Barn, it was five stories high and almost 200 feet long. The towering remains still stand like an Egyptian temple. The site was designated a National Historic Landmark in 1965. The site is open for special viewing days in the summer. Contact the Shaker Museum and Library at Old Chatham, New York, for more information (see below, page 185.)

Sodus Bay — Sodus, New York; 1826–1836

Joseph Pelham and his wife Susanna converted to Shakerism and established a small but prosperous settlement on beautiful Sodus Bay in western New York State in 1826. It was a convenient way station for Shakers who were traveling to and from the western Shaker communities. In 1836, the Shakers reluctantly sold the land to avoid the threat of eminent domain, as a canal was planned for the area. The members, their possessions, livestock, and even the bodies of deceased Shakers were moved to a new settlement called Groveland.

Groveland — Sonyea, New York; 1836–1895

For a while the transplanted Sodus Bay settlement flourished at Groveland, also called Sonyea, but a series of disastrous fires, financial woes, and a lack of new converts finally led to its closing. The site was sold to New York State to be used as the Craig Colony for Epileptics. Later, the property was transferred to the New York State Department of Corrections and turned into a maximum security prison. A few Shaker buildings remain, some surrounded by fences and barbed wire, but none of the buildings are open to the public.

For an interesting article on Sodus Bay and Groveland, see the website of *The Crooked Lake Review*, a local historical quarterly magazine for central and western New York State. This article may be found at *http://www.crookedlakereview.com/books/saints_sinners/martin6.html.*

OHIO

Union Village — Lebanon, Ohio; 1806–1912

In the early 1800s, Shakers sent missionaries west to seek new converts. In the wilds of Ohio, then the frontier, the early Shakers tried unsuccessfully to convert Native Americans who still lived nearby. They had better luck with Methodist and Presbyterian communities, and eventually organized four Shaker communities in Ohio.

The first settlement was originally called Turtle Creek and then renamed Union Village. As at some other sites, local residents distrusted the Shakers and threatened them with violence. But eventually, Union Village thrived, becoming home to more than 400 Shakers. It was an important site, the administrative center of the western Shakers.

But as with other Shaker villages, membership inevitably lessened after the Civil War. In the 1890s, the simple Shaker building known as the Trustees' House was extensively remodeled. At great expense, it was turned into a turreted Victorian castle called Marble Hall, a departure from tradition which was highly controversial. Even these modernizations, however, did not bring new converts, and Union Village was doomed to close, the first and last of the Ohio Shaker sites.

The grounds and buildings of Union Village were eventually sold to a religious group which used them as a home for children and the elderly. Marble Hall is now part of a retirement living community but is open to the public during business hours.

Watervliet — *Dayton, Ohio; 1806–1910*

Watervliet was another of the early Shaker communities organized in western Ohio. A Presbyterian congregation in the Beaver Creek area was the nucleus for the Watervliet Shaker community. Watervliet, named for the original settlement established by Mother Ann in New York State, had more than 800 acres, with about 100 members at its peak. The community was known for its chair-making business but also derived income from the sale of garden seeds and farm produce.

As the twentieth century opened, declining membership and dwindling economic resources forced Watervliet to close. The remaining members moved to Union Village, and much of the property was sold to the State of Ohio for a state hospital farm. No Shaker buildings remain at this site.

North Union — *Near Cleveland, Ohio; 1822–1889*

The Shaker community of North Union was established in 1822. When this community closed, the Shakers sold the land to developers who built Shaker Heights, one of the nation's first planned suburban communities. All the Shaker buildings are long since demolished. Foundations for one of the Shaker mills exist and the two small lakes in the park are Shaker-made. The land is a productive archeological site, and public access is restricted in some areas. Some of the small park has walking trails.

The Shaker Historical Museum, on land that was once the North Union apple orchard, is administered by the Ohio Historical Society and operated by the Shaker Historical Society. The Shaker Historical Museum is open to the public and contains Shaker artifacts and photographs of the North Union community. Additional information about the Shaker Historical Society is available at *http://www.shakerhistory.com.*

Whitewater — *New Haven, Ohio; 1824–1907*

The Whitewater community began with only eighteen Believers, but grew to a substantial settlement with three families and 1,400 acres. Shakers from Union Village found converts among the Methodists of this area, and the fertile soil, timberland, and the nearby Whitewater River made this a good place to establish a settlement. As with most other Shaker sites, shrinking membership and economic troubles led to its closure.

Whitewater Shaker Village retains most of its beautiful Shaker buildings in their original settings; about twenty structures remain, which were purchased from their private owners by the Hamilton County Park District in 1989–1991. The Friends of the Whitewater Shaker Village has leased the North Family, including the 1827 Meeting House and 1832 Dwelling House, from the Hamilton County Park District and is developing plans to open it to the public. The village is not open to the public at the present time.

Additional information about Whitewater is available at *http://www.whitewatershakervillage.org/.*

KENTUCKY

Pleasant Hill — *Harrodsburg, Kentucky; 1806–1910*

This beautiful spot is only about seventy-five miles from Abraham Lincoln's birthplace near Hodgenville, and since he lived in Kentucky until 1816, it's possible he saw Pleasant Hill Shakers when he was a child. Pleasant Hill became one of the largest Shaker communities, and at its peak in 1830 was home to approximately 500 Shakers. Once a showplace of agricultural excellence, with prize-winning livestock and thriving crops, it was hard hit economically during the Civil War and never recovered. The community closed in 1910.

Pleasant Hill is now a beautifully restored Shaker site, on 3,000 acres of land, with many excellent examples of Shaker architecture. In the Trustees' Office, twin spiral staircases rise in graceful loops, three stories high. The village is a National Historic Landmark, and is open to the public year round. Additional information about Pleasant Hill is available at *http://www.shakervillageky.org*.

South Union — *South Union, Kentucky; 1807–1922*

The once-thriving community of South Union was frequently harassed by soldiers of both sides during the Civil War. Today, the Shaker Museum at South Union owns many restored Shaker buildings, some of them magnificent examples of Shaker architecture, on 600 acres of original farmland. The museum has an enormous collection of Shaker furniture and artifacts, and offers a wide range of tours and activities year round. Additional information about South Union is available at *http://www.shakermuseum.com*.

INDIANA

West Union — *Knox County, Indiana; 1810–1827*

West Union, also known as Busro, was the westernmost outpost of Shakerism. Three hundred Believers once lived in this village, but the settlement was plagued with difficulties from the start. During the War of 1812, there were threats of Indian attacks or British invasion. The village was sited on swampy river bottomlands, and recurring outbreaks of malaria weakened the members. Bitter disagreements among the Believers hastened the community's end. The settlement dissolved and many members went to Pleasant Hill or other Shaker villages. The collapse of West Union was a disappointment to the Shakers' hopes of western expansion.

Archeological work is sometimes done on the site, but no buildings remain.

GEORGIA

White Oak — *White Oak, Georgia; 1898–1902*

The Shakers continued their hopes of expanding their settlements into warmer climates, and sunk thousands of dollars into buying the land of several antebellum plantations in Georgia. They called their settlement White Oak. "In a beautiful Southern mansion with abundant acreage, timber, fish, sea-breeze, promising fruit, we daily perform our duty, asking God's blessing upon our labors," wrote one Georgia settler.[4]

But few northern Shakers wanted to move south permanently. No new converts came, and the community was soon financially overextended. It rapidly closed and was sold to a private owner. Only a few traces remain.

FLORIDA

Narcoossee — *Ashton, Florida; 1896–1911*

Some Shakers, as the membership aged, began looking for a more comfortable climate, and considered a move south. Believers from Watervliet, New York, purchased land in Florida and established the Narcoossee settlement. While no more than a few lived there at any one time, the colony was for a while quite successful.

Always eager to try new things, the Shaker farmers began to raise unfamiliar crops like sugar cane, sweet potatoes, and bananas, and were famed for their excellent pineapples. "The balmy breezes for the past two months are having a salutary effect upon the fruit trees of Florida," wrote one transplanted Northerner. "To pass through an orchard of one or two thousand trees, and inhale the sweet fragrance, is a thing to gladden the heart."[3]

Though the Shakers were highly respected by their neighbors, no converts joined them. Drought, and the arduous business of clearing the palmetto bush for agriculture, were too much for the few who lived there, and they eventually returned north.

Little remains of the Shakers' buildings at Narcoossee, and the land upon which the settlement was located is now privately owned.

༄

Shaker Museum and Library — *Old Chatham, New York*

The Shaker Museum and Library was founded in 1950 by John S. Williams, Sr., in collaboration with Shakers who were then living at Hancock, Canterbury, and Sabbathday Lake. The museum and library is located at what was Williams' summer home, not a Shaker site, but it is not far from the important Shaker village at Mount Lebanon. The museum houses a vast collection of Shaker furniture, textiles, art, tools, and agricultural machinery — tens of thousands of artifacts and archival items. The museum is open spring through fall, and the library is open by appointment. A wide range of seasonal educational programs and public events are held.

Part of the mission of the Shaker Museum and Library is to preserve and interpret nearby Mount Lebanon Shaker Village for future generations. There are exciting plans for the restoration of Mount Lebanon, in collaboration with the World Monuments Fund and the National Park Service.

Additional information about the Shaker Museum and Library is available at *http://www.shakermuseumandlibrary.org.*

The Shaker Historic Trail

The Shaker Historic Trail, A National Register of Historic Places Travel Itinerary, is a virtual tour of Shaker history, its place within American Utopian societies, and 15 of the larger, more important, and better preserved Shaker village sites in New England,

New York, and the Midwest. The project is a "partnership project produced by the National Park Service's National Register of Historic Places and Northeast Regional Office, in conjunction with the Shaker communities and museums of the east coast and the National Conference of State Historic Preservation Officers." To travel the Shaker Historic Trail, to visit the most well-preserved Shaker sites, and to review a wealth of other information about Shakers and their times, visit *http://www.nps.gov/nr/travel/shaker/ index.htm.*

Notes

[1] There is some discrepancy in the sources as to the year a Shaker community officially began or ended. It's sometimes difficult to date precisely when a village was "gathered into order," and occasionally the land remained in the Shakers' possession long after the last Shaker left the premises. The dates provided in this listing for the beginning and ending of Shaker settlements are those given in John T. Kirk, *The Shaker World: Art, Life, Belief,* New York, NY: Harry N. Abrams, Inc., 1997.

[2] Taylor and White, *Shakerism,* p. 137.

[3] *The Manifesto,* March 1899, vol. 29, no. 3.

[4] *The Manifesto,* October 1899, vol. 29, no. 10, p. 160.

Bibliography

Alcott, Louisa May. *Hospital Sketches*. Bedford, MA: Applewood Books, 1993. First published in 1863.

———. *Transcendental Wild Oats*. Harvard, MA: The Harvard Common Press, 1975. First published in 1873.

Anonymous. *The History of Warren County, Ohio*. Chicago, IL: W. H. Beers and Co., 1882. Available at *www.rootsweb.ancestry.com/~ohwarren/*, the website of OHGenWeb.

———. *In Memoriam: Henry C. Blinn, 1824–1905*. Concord, NH: Rumford Printing Co., 1905. Contains *Autobiographical Notes* by Henry Blinn.

Andrews, Edward Deming. *The Gift to Be Simple: Songs, Dances and Rituals of the Shakers*. New York, NY: Dover Publications, 1962.

———. *The People Called Shakers*. New York, NY: Dover Publications, Inc., 1963.

Andrews, Edward Deming, and Faith Andrews. *Shaker Furniture: The Craftsmanship of an American Communal Sect*. New York, NY: Dover Publications, Inc., 1950.

———. *Religion in Wood: A Book of Shaker Furniture*. Bloomington, IN: Indiana University Press, 1982.

———. *Work and Worship Among the Shakers: Their Craftsmanship and Economic Order*. New York, NY: Dover Publications, 1982.

Barker, Mildred R. *Holy Land: A History of the Alfred Shakers*. Sabbathday Lake, ME: The Shaker Press, 1986.

Bishop, Rufus, and Seth Youngs Wells, compilers. *Testimonies of the Life, Character, Revelations and Doctrines of Our Ever Blessed Mother Ann Lee, and the Elders with Her; through whom the Word of Eternal Life was Opened in this Day of Christ's Second Appearing: Collected from Living Witnesses, by Order of the Ministry, in Union with the Church*. Hancock, MA: J. Tallcott and J. Deming, 1816.

Blinn, Henry. *An Historical Record of the Society of Believers in Canterbury, N. H., vols. 1 and 2*, 1892. In the collection of Canterbury Shaker Village, Canterbury, NH.

————. *Life and Gospel Experience of Mother Ann Lee.* Canterbury, NH: Published by the Shakers, 1901.

Bowen, Ezra, editor. *This Fabulous Century.* Morristown, NJ: Time/Life Books, Silver Burdett Co., 1970.

Bradford, Roderick. *D. M. Bennett: The Truth Seeker.* Amherst, NY: Prometheus Books, 2006.

Bradford, William. *Of Plymouth Plantation.* New York, NY: Random House, 1981. First published in 1856 as *History of Plymouth Plantation.*

Brewer, Priscilla J. *Shaker Communities, Shaker Lives.* Hanover, NH: University Press of New England, 1986.

Brock, Peter. *Pacifism in the United States From the Colonial Era to the First World War.* Princeton, NJ: Princeton University Press, 1968.

Brooks, Noah. *Lincoln Observed: Civil War Dispatches of Noah Brooks.* Baltimore, MD: The Johns Hopkins University Press, 1998.

Burns, Deborah. *Shaker Cities of Peace, Love and Union.* Hanover, NH: University Press of New England, 1993.

Burrows, Edwin G., and Mike Wallace. *Gotham: A History of New York City to 1898.* New York, NY: Oxford University Press, 1999.

Carr, Frances. *Growing Up Shaker.* Sabbathday Lake, ME: United Society of Shakers, 1995.

Catton, Bruce. *Never Call Retreat.* New York, NY: Simon and Schuster, Inc., 1967.

————. *This Hallowed Ground: The Union Side of the Civil War.* Garden City, NY: Doubleday and Company, Inc., 1955.

Central Ministry Journal, 1859–1874. New Lebanon, NY. In the collection of the Shaker Museum and Library, Old Chatham, NY.

Cheever, Susan. *American Bloomsbury: Louisa May Alcott, Ralph Waldo Emerson, Margaret Fuller, Nathaniel Hawthorne, and Henry David Thoreau: Their Lives, Their Loves, Their Work.* New York, NY: Simon and Schuster, Inc., 2006.

Clark, Thomas D. *Pleasant Hill in the Civil War.* Lexington, KY: Pleasant Hill Press, 1972.

Cohen, Joel, editor. *Simple Gifts: Shaker Chants and Spirituals* A Recording of Shaker Music by the Shakers of Sabbathday Lake and the Boston Camerata. 1 Audio CD, Erato Disques, 1995. Liner notes written by Sister Frances Carr and Joel Cohen.

Coles, Harold L. *The War of 1812.* Chicago, IL: The University of Chicago Press, 1965.

Cummins, Roger William. "The Second Eden: Charles Lane and American Transcendentalism." Master's thesis, The University of Minnesota, 1967.

Dickinson, Rodolphus. *A Compilation of the Laws of Massachusetts.* Boston, MA: Bradford and Read, 1811.

Donald, David Herbert. *Lincoln.* New York, NY: Simon and Schuster, 1995.

Evans, Frederick William. *Ann Lee (The Founder of the Shakers): A Biography.* Albany, NY: Charles van Benthuysen and Sons, 1858.

———. *Autobiography of a Shaker, and Revelation of the Apocalypse.* New York, NY: American News Co., 1888.

Francis, Richard. *Ann the Word.* New York, NY: Arcade Publishing, 2001.

Garrett, Clarke. *From the Old World to the New World: Origins of the Shakers.* Baltimore, MD: Johns Hopkins University Press, 1987.

Gibran, Kahlil. *The Prophet.* New York, NY: Alfred A. Knopf, 2002.

Gilmore, James R. *Personal Recollections of Abraham Lincoln and the Civil War.* Mechanicsburg, PA: Stackpole Books, 2007. First published in 1898.

Gladwell, Malcolm. *The Tipping Point.* Boston, MA: Little, Brown and Co., 2000.

Goodwillie, Christian, editor. *Shaker Songs: A Celebration of Peace, Harmony, and Simplicity.* New York, NY: Black Dog & Leventhal Publishers, Inc., 2002.

Grant, Jerry V., and Douglas R. Allen. *Shaker Furniture Makers.* Hanover, NH: University Press of New England, 1989.

Holzer, Harold. *Dear Mr. Lincoln; Letters to the President.* Reading, MA: Addison-Wesley Publishing Company, 1993.

———. *Lincoln at Cooper Union.* New York, NY: Simon and Schuster, 2004.

Holzer, Harold, editor. *The Lincoln Mailbag: America Writes to the President, 1861–1865.* Carbondale, IL: Southern Illinois University Press, 1998.

Horgan, Edward R. *The Shaker Holy Land: A Community Portrait.* Boston, MA: The Harvard Common Press, 1987.

Hunt, Gaillard. *As We Were: Life in America in 1814.* Stockbridge, MA: Berkshire House Publishers, 1993. First published in 1914 as *Life in America One Hundred Years Ago.*

Jackson, Rebecca. *Gifts of Power: The Writings of Rebecca Jackson, Black Visionary, Shaker Eldress,* Jean McMahon Humez, editor. Amherst, MA: University of Massachusetts Press, 1987.

Jefferson, Thomas. *The Life and Selected Writings of Thomas Jefferson,* Adrienne Koch and William Peden, editors. New York, NY: Random House, Inc., 1944.

Kirk, John T. *The Shaker World: Art, Life, Belief.* New York, NY: Harry N. Abrams, Inc., 1997.

Klein, Maury. *Days of Defiance: Sumter, Secession and the Coming of the Civil War.* New York, NY: Alfred A. Knopf, Inc., 1997.

Koomler, Sharon D. *Shaker Style.* London, UK: PRC Publishing, Ltd., 2000.

Lankford, Nelson. *Cry Havoc! The Crooked Road to the Civil War, 1861.* New York, NY: Viking Press, 2007.

Lindsay, Bertha. *Seasoned with Grace; My Generation of Shaker Cooking.* Woodstock, VT: The Countryman Press, 1987.

Livermore, Thomas L. *Numbers and Losses in the Civil War in America, 1861–1865.* Bloomington, IN: Indiana University Press, 1957. First published in 1900.

MacLean, J. P. *Shakers of Ohio.* Columbus, OH: F. J. Heer Printing Co., 1907.

The Manifesto, February, 1899, vol. 29, no. 2; March, 1899, vol. 29, no. 3; October, 1899, vol. 29, no. 10. (This periodical was called *The Shaker Manifesto* from 1878–1882.)

Melcher, Marguerite. *The Shaker Adventure. A History of the Shakers from the Eighteenth Century to the Twentieth.* Old Chatham, NY: The Shaker Museum, 1986.

Miller, Amy Bess. *Shaker Medicinal Herbs: A Compendium of History, Lore, and Uses.* New York, NY: N. Potter, Inc., 1976.

Moore, Nancy. *The Journal of Eldress Nancy Moore.* Mary Julia Neal, editor. Nashville, TN: The Parthenon Press, 1963.

Morse, Flo. *Shakers and the World's People.* New York, NY: Dodd, Mead, and Co., 1980.

Moser, Thomas. *How to Build Shaker Furniture.* New York, NY: Sterling Publishing Co., Inc., 1977.

Muller, Charles R., and Timothy D. Rieman. *The Shaker Chair.* Atglen, PA: Schiffer Publishing, Ltd., 2003.

Murdock, Eugene C. *One Million Men: The Civil War Draft in the North.* Worcester, MA: Heffernan Press Inc., 1971.

Murray, Stuart. *Shaker Heritage Guidebook.* Spencertown, NY: Golden Hill Press, 1994.

Nicolay, John G. *A Short Life of Abraham Lincoln.* New York, NY: The Century Company, 1902.

Oates, Stephen B. *Our Fiery Trial: Abraham Lincoln, John Brown, and the Civil War Era.* Amherst, MA: University of Massachusetts Press, 1979.

Ott, John Harlow. *Hancock Shaker Village: A Guidebook and History.* Hancock, MA: Shaker Community, Inc., 1976.

Patterson, Daniel. *The Shaker Spiritual.* Mineola, NY: Dover Publications, Inc., 2000.

Pennino-Baskerville, Mary. "Terpsichore Reviled: Antidance Tracts in Elizabethan England." *Sixteenth Century Journal 1991,* vol. 22, no. 3, pp. 475–493.

Phelps, Lillian. *Shaker Music; A Brief History.* Canterbury, NH: Published by the Canterbury Shakers.

Piercy, Caroline. *A Shaker Cookbook: Not by Bread Alone.* New York, NY: Crown Publishers, Inc., 1953.

Pittsfield Sun, August 29, 1861.

Randolph, Sallie G., and Nancy O'Keefe Bolick. *Shaker Inventions.* New York, NY: Walker and Co., 1990.

Ray, Delia. *Behind the Blue and Gray: The Soldier's Life in the Civil War.* New York, NY: Scholastic Inc., 1991.

Records of the South Family of the United Society, called Shakers, in the town of Watervliet, Albany County and State of New York, July 4, 1830–Dec 13, 1887. In the collection of the Shaker Heritage Society, Albany, NY.

Rieman, Timothy D. *Shaker Furniture: A Craftsman's Journal.* Atglen, PA: Schiffer Publishing, 2006.

Rieman, Timothy D., and Jean M. Burks. *The Complete Book of Shaker Furniture.* New York, NY: Harry N. Abrams, Inc., 1993.

Robinson, Charles Edson. *The Shakers and Their Homes.* Canterbury, NH: Shaker Village, Inc. and New Hampshire Publishing Co., 1976.

Schecter, Barnet. *The Devil's Own Work: The Civil War Draft Riots and the Fight to Reconstruct America.* New York, NY: Walker and Co., 2005.

Schlissel, Lillian. *Conscience in America: A Documentary History of Conscientious Objection in America, 1757 to 1967.* New York, NY: E. P. Dutton and Co., Inc., 1968.

Sears, Clara Endicott. *Gleanings from Shaker Journals.* Boston, MA: Houghton Mifflin Co., 1916.

The Shaker Manifesto, March, 1880, vol. 10, no. 3; June, 1881 vol. 11, no. 6. (See also *The Manifesto,* above.)

Shaver, Elizabeth, and Ned Pratt. *The Watervliet Shakers and Their 1848 Meeting House.* Albany, NY: The Shaker Heritage Society, 1994.

Sheldon, George. *When the Smoke Cleared at Gettysburg.* Nashville, TN: Cumberland House Publishing, Inc., 2003.

Sloane, Eric. *A Reverence for Wood.* New York, NY: Funk and Wagnalls, Inc., 1965.

———. *An Age of Barns: An Illustrated Review of Classic Barn Styles and Construction.* Stillwater, MN: Voyageur Press, 2001.

Sprigg, June. *By Shaker Hands.* Hanover, NH: University Press of New England, 1975.

———. *Simple Gifts; Lessons in Living From a Shaker Village.* New York, NY: Vintage Books, 1998.

Sprigg, June, and David Larkin. *Shaker Life, Work and Art.* New York, NY: Smithmark Publishers, 2000.

Stein, Stephen. *The Shaker Experience in America.* New Haven, CT: Yale University Press, 1992.

Swank, Scott T. *Canterbury Shaker Village.* Lawrenceburg, IN: R. L. Ruehrwein, Publisher, 2003.

Taylor, Frank G. "An Analysis of Shaker Education: The Life and Death of an Alternative Educational System 1774–1950," Doctoral dissertation, University of Connecticut, 1976.

Taylor, Leila S. *A Memorial to Eldress Anna White and Elder Daniel Offord*. Mount Lebanon, NY: North Family of the Shakers, 1912.

Tollefson, James W. *The Strength Not to Fight: Conscientious Objectors of the Vietnam War*. Washington, DC: Brassey's, Inc., 2000.

White, Anna, and Leila S. Taylor. *Shakerism: Its Meaning and Message*. Columbus, OH: Press of Fred J. Heer, 1905.

White, Ronald C. *Lincoln's Greatest Speech: The Second Inaugural*. New York, NY: Simon and Schuster, 2002.

Williams, Richard E. *Called and Chosen; the Story of Mother Rebecca Jackson and the Philadelphia Shakers*. Metuchen, NJ: The Scarecrow Press, Inc., and The American Theological Library Association, 1981.

Wilson, Rufus Rockwell. *Intimate Memories of Lincoln*. Elmira, NY: The Primavera Press, 1945.

Witcher, Mary. *Mary Witcher's Shaker Housekeeper*. New Gloucester, ME: The Shaker Society, 1998. First printed in 1882.

Youngs, Benjamin S., and Calvin Green. *Testimony of Christ's Second Appearing*. Albany, NY: Van Benthuysen, Printer, 1856.

Acknowledgments

A sincere thank-you to those dedicated Shaker scholars who so helpfully guided me through the maze of Shaker books, maps, journals, and other resources: Tina Agren at Sabbathday Lake Shaker Village, Renee Fox at Canterbury Shaker Village, Christian Goodwillie at Hancock Shaker Village, and Anne Clothier at the Shaker Heritage Society. Thank you to Jerry Grant of the Shaker Museum and Library for much helpful advice, and many wonderful photos.

Darryl Thompson's vivid portrayal of twentieth-century life at Canterbury made the Shakers come alive for me. I am greatly indebted to him for sharing so much of his time as well as his enthusiasm, knowledge, and expertise.

Many thanks to Joan Jobson for her beautiful and painstaking artwork, which has helped me appreciate anew the simple elegance of a Shaker chair. Thanks to Gage Evans, who shared in my first explorations of Hancock and Canterbury, and to Lilly Glatz, who helped me mine for gold in Henry Blinn's journals. Thanks to my great writers' group: Lyn Miller-Lachmann, Deb Livingston Picker, and Linda Marshall for their critiques. Thanks to Lois Miner Huey for her input as well. Many thanks to military historians Joseph Balkoski, Gary Phillips, and Dick Weeks; their insights are much appreciated. Any errors in the book are mine alone.

I would like to offer sincere gratitude to Jerry McDonald of The McDonald & Woodward Publishing Company for his creative and courteous editorial guidance. Many thanks to Trish Newcomb, also of McDonald and Woodward, for all her help and advice.

Endless thanks to my husband, George Steele, who puts up with my frequent staring into space and hours tapping on the computer. Thanks to Alex Steele for, once again, sharpening, polishing, and critiquing with an eagle eye. Thanks to Timothy Steele for his excellent photographic work.

Lastly, my grateful appreciation to the Shakers themselves. Attending a worship service at Sabbathday Lake was an experience I will always remember. Thanks, too, to those Shakers who have passed on, for all the beauty they created, and all that they have taught me.

Index

00431 8146